AFTER 40 YEARS
IT ALL GETS
A BIT VAGUE...

An Uncertain History of the
Eric the Half-A-Brick
Testimonial Pub Crawl

By RENOIR

After 40 Years It All Gets A Bit Vague...
Copyright © **2019 Renoir**
All rights reserved.

ISBN: 978-0-9946174-3-9

Published by **Meredian Pictures & Words 2019**
Ballina, Australia
No parts of this publication may be reproduced, stored in a retrieval system, or transmitted in any form or by any means, electronic, mechanical, photocopying, recording, or otherwise, without the prior written permission of the copyright owner. This book is sold subject to the condition that it shall not, by way of trade or otherwise, be lent, resold, hired out, or otherwise circulated without the publisher's prior consent in any form of binding or cover other than that in which it is published and without a similar condition including this condition being imposed on the subsequent purchaser. Under no circumstances may any part of this book be photocopied for resale.

Dedicated with much more
than fondness
and gratitude to
Ewan
Meredith
Close Personal Friends of
Eric, past and future

and of course, Eric.

By the same author:

The Dubious Magic series:

The Wizard of Waramanga
The Carvings of Cobbemarmoo
The Mad Machines of Mundara
The Warriors of Wiwo'ole
The Spirits of Sron Dubh

For the Young And Old Souls

These Old Bastards...

The Quiet Word series:
Mid-Life Crisis MANagement
(The Bloke's Guide to Surviving Middle Age and Male Menopause)

Move It Like You Mean It
(A Quiet Word About Parkinson's Disease In Men)

Visit www.renoirwords.com

Contained herein...

FOREWORD, and Some Acknowledgements 6

PART ONE: THE FIRST TWENTY-SOMETHING YEARS

1 PRE-HISTORY... BEFORE ERIC WAS ERIC 9

2 IT ALL STARTS HERE – THE GALAH SOCIAL EVENT OF 1979 12

3 THE EARLY YEARS – SUCH AS THEY WERE 18

4 1983 – A CHRISTMAS CRACKER 20

5 1984 – A SMALL CROWD, BUT A HAPPY ONE 24

6 1985 – INCREASING VISIBILITY 27

7 1986 – GETTING OFFICIAL 31

8 1987 – ERIC IN ANOTHER STATE 37

9 1988 – EKSHPO? WHAT EKSHPO? 42

10 88-89 THE SUPPLEMENT 49

11 1989 – ERIC, THE MOVIE 55

12 1990 – A YEAR OF LEGENDS 59

13 1991 – A HERITAGE LOST 63

14 1992 – SCARY! 67

15 1993 – IMAGES 71

16 1994 – MORE SINGIN' IN THE RAIN 74

17 1995 – SMART CASUAL ATTIRE 78

18 1996 – JUDY TAKES CHARGE 81

19 1997 – THE FIRST ADULT ERIC 84

20 1998 – SHOWTIME! 88

21 1999 – TREATING ZYMOCENOSILICAPHOBIA 91

22 2000 – HISTORY IS WRITTEN BY THE SURVIVORS 98

23 LURCH'S STORY 105

24 HOW LONG CAN THIS GO ON? 109

PART TWO: THE NEXT MILLENNIUM

25 NEW THINGS 112

26 2001 – A BRICK'S ODYSSEY 114

27 2002 – AN ODYSSEY OF HOMERIC PROPORTIONS 119

28 2003 - CHALLENGING 123

29 2004 – A STUDY IN SILVER 126

30 2005 - SOMETHING WICKED THIS WAY CRAWLS... 131

31 2006 – THE SOUTH SHALL RISE AGAIN 134

32 2007 – AN ACT OF CHARITY 137

33 2008 – A LITTLE BASTARDRY 141

34 ALASTAIR'S STORY 145

35 2009 – THIRTY, NOT THIRSTY 155

36 2010 – SORRY, I MISSED THAT... 158

37 2011 – CALLING 'TIME' ON THE TANK 160

38 2012 – 33 AND 1/2, SOME KIND OF A RECORD 162

39 2013 – BON VOYAGE 165

40 2014 – ELEVEN ON THE ELEVENTH 168

41 2015 – PUBLICLY TRANSPORTED 171

42 2016 – A BIT UP-MARKET 175

43 2017 – MY DRY RUN 177

44 2018 – SO NEAR AND YET SO FAR 180

45 2019 – THE FORTIETH ANNIVERSARY 182

46 NOT A CONCLUSION 189

FOREWORD, and Some Acknowledgements

I've called this an Uncertain History because there are some parts that are perhaps *conjectural*. That's not to say they didn't happen, but memories aren't as clear as they might be after nearly four decades of annual overindulgence.

What I have has been assembled from photos, diaries, scribbled notes, conversations – whatever sources I could find.. I make no promises about veracity but it's the best I could do. I haven't changed anything or made anything up for the sake of entertainment – frankly, I haven't needed to!

The first part of the book was written in early 2001, before the 22nd Crawl, as a belated marking of the 20th anniversary. (Mostly. I've added a few bits that other good folks have since reminded or told me of.) The second part covers the 'new millennium'. You might notice I've changed a bit as a writer (more practice). There were fewer resources to draw on for a lot of those years – for various reasons memorabilia things weren't kept with quite the same attention. Some years draw a total blank in my memory, although I *know* we didn't miss any. Social media has filled a few gaps, and I've drawn things together as quickly as I can: I didn't want to be late for the second twenty years!

There are quite a lot of people without whom this story could never have been told, no matter how you look at it.

It could never have been told without the participation of Pub Crawlers – the *Close Personal Friends of Eric* – numbering by now in the hundreds after all these years. To all of them, I say thanks for the fun.

It could never have been told without the love and forbearance of four very special ladies over the years: Helen, Gill, Julie and for the last nine years Meredith. To all of them I say thanks for the love, support and patience.

It could never have been told without the efforts of a succession of medical practitioners and specialists around the country who've kept my body going despite the abuses I've heaped upon it – only some of which are detailed herein.

It could never have been told if the Bjelke-Petersen government of 1979 hadn't been such appalling cultural vandals. I'm *not* going to thank them for that, even though we've made a rather impressive silk purse from their sow's ear.

It could never have been told without the memory-jogging photographs of people such as Judy Fogarty, Matt Taylor, Adam Cretier, Gregor Shevtzoff, Val Weatherley, Sharon Benson, Michael McPartland, Colleen Rossi and probably others who I've forgotten took particular snaps. My thanks to you all.

It could have been told, but far less effectively, without the contributions (written and spoken) of Ewan Logan, Karl Johnston, Mark Moore, Robbo, Alastair Wallace, Paul Kalluschke, Marc and Wayne Hunter and Dallas Scriven. I like Karl's comment after apologizing for one or two question marks:
The rest is remarkably accurate. I'm good with moments – it's the years I forget.
Their memories have added a great deal to my own – thanks, guys.

Thanks too, to Ian Mansell, for finding the old Hansard records that gave me a framework for Chapter 1. And to Mike O'Connor for kindly giving me permission to quote from his 1985 and 86 Eye Q columns in the Telegraph.

And thanks to you, because if you're reading this it means you're interested in the story of a little half-brick and the catalogue of fun that's grown up around him. That makes you a part of this history too.

Welcome aboard, and cheers!

.o0o.

PART ONE: THE FIRST TWENTY-SOMETHING YEARS

1 PRE-HISTORY... BEFORE ERIC WAS ERIC

It all starts with a pub. Well of course it does – it's a Pub Crawl! But it starts with a pub that has never been visited during any of the events recalled in most of this book, except in spirit.

The Belle Vue Hotel was built around 1885, on the corner of Alice and George Streets in Brisbane, providing fine hospitality in the Parliamentary Precinct. The guest book over the years featured royalty (including the mother of the current British Queen for those of you of a monarchist persuasion), visiting stars like Ava Gardner, and, inevitably, politicians from Sir Robert Menzies through to generations of Queensland MPs.

One of the last of these was Des Frawley – National Party member for Caboolture – who recalled a particularly windy night in 1978 when he "thought the building would fall down". The poor chap said that he was "so terrified that the Honourable Member for Toowoomba North (Dr. John Lockwood) had to attend to me."

Perhaps it was Mr. Frawley's recollection of his delicate constitution that provoked his enthusiastic support for the final fate of the old Belle Vue.

The Queensland Government bought the Hotel in 1973 for about $600,000. By November of that year the adjacent trees that had added both shade and beauty were removed. The paint was peeling and some of the verandah floors were lifting by early '74, so the response in June of that year was to remove the cast iron lacework that gave the place so much of its charm.

By February 1979 what was left of the verandahs looked pretty shabby, so they were removed. It was the beginning of the end. The best of the fittings – stained glass and woodwork – started to quietly disappear. Some pieces are known to have turned up in posh houses in the wealthy suburb of Hamilton. All purchased quite legitimately, I'm sure.

Premier Bjelke-Petersen said that the Belle Vue was a heap of rubbish that should be bulldozed at the earliest opportunity. In Parliament on April 4 Des Frawley was strident in his agreement with his leader's opinion, as were other luminaries such as Bruce Bishop and Don Lane (the later-disgraced Cabinet Minister, not the TV personality).

The only minor problem was public opinion. The Building Workers' Industrial Union were threatening 'green bans', National Trust members were wringing their hands, and ordinary Brisbane-ites were ringing their talk-back radio stations.

The solution was obvious (to someone) – avoid the glare of publicity by doing the job at night! Shortly before midnight on Friday April 20 1979, the heavy equipment of local legends the Deen Brothers (not to be confused with comedy legends the Dodgy Brothers) began to be unloaded from their trucks at the rear entrance of the Belle Vue, off William Street. Under police guard they set to their destructive work at 12:20 a.m. on Saturday April 21. By sunrise, most of the beloved pub was gone.

The Deens were no strangers to controversy, but have always remained cheerfully indifferent to public opinion. *"All we leave are memories"* is actually their business motto.

There were about 200 protestors who had been keeping an eye on the place in shifts. We vaguely feared that Premier Joh was capable of anything. Sometimes you just hate being right. There was nothing we could do, though.

Nine people, including former breakfast DJ "Wayney-Poo" Roberts, were arrested when their emotions got the better of them and they got into a futile confrontation with the police. Perhaps surprisingly I wasn't one of them.

The Anglican Dean of Brisbane chaired a rally and prayer meeting in the nearby grounds of what was then the QIT (now the grander Queensland University of Technology). We had a small win, as one of the front end loaders burned out something in its motor while trying to dislodge a particularly stubborn section of wall.

But that was a fleeting moment of triumph amidst a lost battle. The original French doors that had somehow avoided being stripped earlier – fine timber and glass – splintered and crashed to the ground amongst shattered masonry.

I stood across George Street, as angry and powerless as the rest. This was a PUB, damn it! It had history, and character, and the right to a future, which should have included my drinking in it!

At about one in the morning a section of front wall came down with considerable force, sending a cloud of debris into the air. As the shower of shattered building fell, half a brick sailed over the hastily-erected protective wire fence, bounced twice on the George Street bitumen, and came to rest at my feet.

Resisting the urge to immediately lob it at the head of the nearest Deen brother, I held on to the little fragment of history.

"I'm meant to have this," I thought.

.o0o.

2 IT ALL STARTS HERE – THE GALAH SOCIAL EVENT OF 1979

The little relic of the Belle Vue had a name virtually straight away. Any Monty Python fan should recognise that half-an-anything should automatically be called Eric.

For the benefit of non-Pythonists, and those too young to know, the derivation is briefly as follows: in a memorable sketch, a typical Python loony seeks a licence for his pet cat, Eric. It transpires that he has a whole menagerie of critters all named Eric, including a half-bee, which leads into a wonderful nonsense song about Eric, the Half-a-Bee.

See? Simple, really.

Pythonism was an important part of my life at the time. So too was drinking, often to excess. In the course of an inebriated conversation a few of us decided that a belated wake for the Belle Vue was a good idea.

An even better idea – let's make it a Pub Crawl! And let's take Eric with us. If you can't bring Mohammed to the mountain, take the mountain to Mohammed. If we can't drink in the Belle Vue any more, we'll take the Belle Vue to for a drink everywhere else!

Saturday September 8 was chosen for the "**Galah Social Event of 1979**". That's what it said on the official invitation.

Quite a few people expressed their enthusiasm for the idea, so the above-mentioned official invite was whipped up, from *J. B. Scotland and the miraculous Budgie*. Those were the nicknames by which yours truly and Bill Meyers were known in those days.

A primitive 'wet copy' photocopier in the Accounts Payable unit of Australia Post produced a number of dodgy grey copies, of which as far as I'm aware only one remains.

While I was in the employ of Australia Post, Eric gained a little extra notoriety when he was photographed dressed as Santa for the staff newsletter. He had a fake beard and a sweet little red hat. What could you expect from someone who actually was entered onto the payroll (without pay, of course!) as a Class 1 Conversation Piece – Acting Paperweight Duties.

Unlike pretty much every event afterwards, that first Crawl had rules other than "There are no rules." Sort of. They went like this:

The rules are simple:
1. *One pot per pub.*
2. *Everyone buys their own beer*
   (At an average of 50c a pot, those planning to complete the course best bring about $15-$20)
   It's not a competition (except maybe a personal test of ability), it's just a fun event.

Yes. 50 cents a pot. Some were as cheap as 40c, others made us wince at nearly 90c in the posh bars. Of course, we were all earning rather less in a month than today's average weekly wage...

The scheduled route on the invitation was:

Railway	Transcontinental	Majestic
Grosvenor	Crest	Plaza
Criterion	York	Carlton
Her Majesty's	Embassy	Arcadia
Treasury	George	Port Office
Exchange	Victory	Grand
Queens	Belfast	National
Orient	Brisbane	Central
(and if we get this far...) Federal		Sportsman
Leichhardt	Alliance	St. Pauls.

We were nothing if not ambitious!

Of that impressive list I think only ten names remain. In some cases the name is the same but the bar is unrecognizable. In other cases, some sort of licenced premises occupy the same address, but the identity has certainly changed.

Despite the professed enthusiasm, there were only four starters on the day. Budgie and I were joined by Ewan 'Ern' Logan and Ian Cuthbert, better known as Cleo. Ern's thoughts and recollections are recorded later in this chapter, a contribution for which I'm profoundly grateful.

It's funny how, so many years on, quite different things have stuck in our respective memories. Ern mentions things I'd forgotten, while I recall incidents he'd lost in the haze of the past. A handful of rough photos also help!

As we walked up Ann Street from the Crest, dragging Eric behind us in a plastic sled made from an old Polaroid camera box, we were stopped by two members of the constabulary who demanded to know what we were doing with "that... that... *thing*" (indicating Eric). As Cleo attempted to explain the occasion, Ern noticed that neither of the officers was wearing the name badges that recent regulations required them to display. This prompted him to announce to the offending policemen that he was making a Citizen's Arrest.

While the police threatened to arrest us for disturbing the peace, and Ern threatened to arrest the police, we were being observed by Barbara, the wife of my Medieval Drama lecturer. By chance, she and her mother were sitting at the nearby bus stop.

Affronted by the threat to our civil liberties, this charming but formidable middle-aged English lady waded into the confrontation, loudly berating the bemused policemen for "picking on these lovely young lads and their pet brick."

With his command of the situation slipping rapidly, a spluttering young constable demanded "Madam's name" as well as all of ours. At this point Barbara's elderly but seriously feisty mother joined the party. Brandishing her umbrella she abused the policeman for accusing her daughter of being a madam.

Clearly this was not a situation covered at the Queensland Police Academy. Sweating, confused and embarrassed, the policemen jumped back into their car, warned us all that they never wanted to see any of us again (including the bloody brick), and took off at speed. Barbara and her Mum graciously declined our invitation to accompany us on the rest of the Crawl.

I have a photo that suggests I decided to have a little lie down in the middle of the intersection outside the Embassy Hotel. I don't remember it. Perhaps I liked the look of the object serving as my pillow – an old 'silent copper', a speed discouraging device probably unknown to any of you under fifty.

Sometime after that we visited the old Belle Vue site, and called in to the QIT Students' Club. I remember bean bags, instant coffee and presumably more beers. Beyond that I'm not sure, but after nearly forty years it all gets a bit vague.

I'll hand over to Ern for his story.

Maybe it started with that bastard Bjelke-Petersen. I don't think many people who actually cared about human rights weren't hassled, if not arrested by the wallopers in those days. A group of three could be considered an illegal assembly if I remember correctly. Yet though corruption reached up to the highest levels in that time, there were still a lot of decent banana-benders. The first Eric was one of THOSE sort of benders.

Eric of course remembers the Railway Hotel. Is it indicative of something that Police HQ now stands where that wonderful stained glass peacock window used to cast its aura of beauty over travellers and other thirsty pilgrims?

Maybe I arrived early, but I seem to recall drinking alone and wondering if anyone else would turn up. I think I'd had a pot before Budgie showed up, but we were certainly a trilogy in four parts (five including Eric) by the time we decided no-one else was going to appear.

Cleo, Renoir (as he's now known), Budgie and Ern – BENT on some serious drinking. Reputedly this is nothing uncommon a latterday Eric (which is a much more elaborate affair) but we only stopped when we ran out of time and hotels. No pleasant ferry rides for the inaugural Crawlers – possibly because we didn't think of it and possibly because of a fear of mixing seasickness with acute alcoholic poisoning.

I honestly don't remember if it was 21 or 23 pubs in each of which we drained a pot, but I seem to recall being somewhere down towards Alice Street banging on the door of a hotel only to find that it was now operated by the Salvo's – bless 'em. Maybe we were trying to embellish the Crawl with a nip of holy spirit, but I don't think I could have coped with communion wine so I suppose it's good that they didn't open the door.

(I'm not sure that the Salvo's do wine, being serious abstainers. The Jesuits do a nice line in altar wines, I'm told – *Renoir*)

The victuals for the Crawl don't really linger in the memory – I suspect it was a liquid lunch, but I think we put some solids into our systems spur of the momentish after sundown at the Treasury. Could it really have been toasted sandwiches with the plastic bags melting on to the bread, with us so famished we consumed the lot anyway? Tell that to the young people today an they WON'T believe you...

I distinctly remember the fearless, intrepid roving reporter Cleo, tape recorder in hand, interviewing total strangers in several establishments as to their thoughts about the ablution facilities. One such interview was in the Grosvenor, later stripped of its immaculate stainless steel "Swedish modern" bar and converted to a Mc-outpost of American cultural imperialism. Admittedly if you've only got a small number of dollars the coffee's passable and cheap if you get a couple of refills.

(Not a lot of consolation for laying a kitchen floor smack on top of the historic first well sunk in Brisbane. *Renoir*)

Another sad story in the destruction of the rural ambience of Brisbane is the disappearance of not only Her Majesty's Theatre, but also Her bar.

Two steps off Queen Street and there you were with your thirst quencher, sheltered from Shakespeare's gaze by a generous awning, although I suspect there would have been something of a smile on his face. All that greets you now as you approach the site would have made Albert Speer proud.

Other icons of our beautiful big country town (now "Australia's greatest city" according to some bullshit artist) have gone the Philistine way. There was the National, where Frog and I saw another departed Brizzie icon the Go-Betweens play live – wasn't it a great venue? There was the York, and the Carlton, whose facades at least were spared to remind us that Brisbane was once a beautiful city before the cankerous Coalition tyranny destroyed it.

Perhaps that destruction began with the stabbing in the back of the gracious old Belle Vue in the dark of the night. Yet Eric, despite decades of an annual bender (and can't he hold his grog?) remembers these places perhaps more vividly than any of us. If only he could talk. Maybe by the end of the latest Crawl you will think you can hear him.

Ern's right about many of his reflections. Looking back over the pictures taken since 1979 I can see so many changes to the faces of my friends, and to the face of Brisbane. Not all of the buildings that have gone were beautiful, but most were in some way at least interesting, and all of them held memories for someone. The city is poorer for their absence.

In chapters to come I'll mention other bars that have vanished or lost their identity. The Crawl itineraries have become something of a sad record of successive losses, and I find myself a diarist of Brisbane's disappearing heritage.

But we don't let ourselves get too depressed by such solemn musings as we take Eric on his annual outing. We're what Rhys Hanson once described as a "big mobile party". Notwithstanding the emotional night that really started it all, since September '79 we've remained true to the promise of that first invitation: a fun event!

.o0o.

3 THE EARLY YEARS – SUCH AS THEY WERE

The grand tradition of Eric Pub Crawls almost died before it was decently established. After the small turnout of '79 there was no great enthusiasm to have another go in 1980.

By 1981 though, a new ad hoc social group had been formed: The North Yeronga Wino Society And Synchronous Gumbies Club. Again, there's that connection with alcohol and Monty Python.

That august body could probably give rise to a book of its own, if anyone could believe some of the things written in in the regular Journal! Suffice to say that the membership fluctuated and varied over time. Among the more reliable (?) attendees were yours truly, my then wife Helen, Budgie, Judy Fogarty (usually known in those days as Frog), and Robbo.

Probably devised after a rousing singing of the Half-a-Bee song, the *plan* was to hold a Crawl to coincide with a significant date of Robbo's that he doesn't talk about (rhymes with Earth Way). Saturday June 6 was the appointed day, and the Transcontinental Hotel the designated launch pad.

It was chaos from the start. Robbo arrived slightly late, to find no-one else there. Frog and her friend Louise arrived, so Robbo headed off down George Street to look for everyone/anyone else, while the girls waited for stragglers. In straggled Helen and I carrying Eric (we'd been delayed waiting for a plumber – I recall jokes about waterworks problems before the Crawl had even started), and after a quick round of drinks we set off in pursuit of the Earth Way boy.

We never did find Robbo again that day.

Budgie found us though, shortly after which Louise left. I don't think those two occurrences were connected.

We managed a complete tour of all of the city's XXXX hotels. No, youngsters, that's not a rating of sexual explicitness. In those days nearly all pubs were operated by Castlemaine Perkins (XXXX – hooray!) or Carlton & United (yah, boo!). The dividing lines were clear, and you grew up with strong, if not necessarily rational loyalties, which for some of us still persist.

Possibly the presence of ladies as 50% or better of the complement was responsible for the beer intake being intersorted with a range of other options. I seem to recall wine and various cocktails during the course of the day. Certainly at the end of the crawl 'proper' all four of us, (Helen and I, Frog and Budgie) dashed home, put Eric in a safe place, got changed into 'better' clothes, and reconvened in Wilson's 1870 Wine Bar.

Wilson's is another lost icon. It was a frequently smoky piano bar downstairs under the now-demolished York Hotel, which stood on one of the sites overrun by the sprawling Myer Centre on Queen Street.

Wine and later pancakes made a particularly civilized ending to the day. We can't have been sober, but the photos taken during the evening show us looking only slightly silly as we tried for casual elegance. I wish I could still fit into that cream satin shirt with the gold trim!

It was only a small event, but it did at least keep the flame flickering.

By my recollection 1982 was another drought, but I suspect Cleo and Robbo may have undertaken a Crawl of their own. Eric would have been with them in spirit.

It took until 1983 for the small flickers to erupt into something that was big enough to take on a life of its own.

.o0o.

4 1983 – A CHRISTMAS CRACKER

I recognize now that late December is, frankly, a bloody stupid time to hold a Pub Crawl in Brisbane. It's far too hot, and everyone has already spent far too much money on Christmas.

Nonetheless, it took us most of the year to get ourselves organized enough to have the 1983 Eric Testimonial.

December 21 saw the starters assemble at 'The Villa' on Dorchester Street, Highgate Hill. This block of four units was home to Helen and I, upstairs from The Two Michaels – not Ronnies – Pegg and Perisic.

Michael Pegg and I were joined by Buddy Doyle, Rhys Hanson, Peter (Jack) Dempsey, and Niall Hamilton. We set off for our starting point, the Melbourne Hotel, with Eric in a little wooden wagon loaned to us for the occasion.

I had a small cassette player with me, and was playing the Blues Brothers version of *Peter Gunn* as travelling music, at as loud a volume as the poor little machine would allow (which wasn't much – it was no ghetto blaster!). I also kept a recording of some of the day's proceedings. Some of it is gibberish – there were too many times I hadn't noticed I'd pressed the *Record* button, but a few gems are revealed.

It seems we set a bit of a cracking pace. There were quite lengthy walks from the Melbourne to the Coronation, and then a half hour traipse across the William Jolly Bridge to get to the Transcontinental, by which time we'd sweated out most of the alcohol of the first two stops.

Looking back I'm rather sorry that the old Coronation only made one official appearance on an Eric Crawl. (In its guise as a Backpackers Hostel it accommodated a couple of interstaters years later, but that's another Chapter.) The Coro was a classical old pub with the traditional wrought iron verandahs now almost completely vanished from the environs of Brisbane's CBD. Tucked away in a corner of the old industrial part of West End, it declined as the passing trade was routed away, up and over the Grey Street Bridge. Expo-driven displacement of many long standing South Brisbane and West End businesses apparently drove the last nail into the Coro's coffin.

At the time though, it didn't mean much to us. I made the comment, "Not a bad pub if you like this sort of thing. Mind you, normally you have to be at least 45 to like this sort of thing." Oops – now I'm showing my age, and then some!

Coming out of the Transcontinental 'the boys' met up with Michael Perisic and 'the girls' – Judy (then still called Frog), Pam who worked in the Bank with Judy, Catherine Collins, and Catherine's small son Aaron, the actual owner of Eric's wagon.

We also were soon to discover as we were making our way along George Street we were being steadily pursued by Lyola Rogers and Toni von Finglebumm-Smythe.

Following our trail from the Melbourne, they'd dash into a bar and the following conversation repeatedly ensued:
"Have you seen..."
"The Brick? They went that way."
One quick drink per bar later they were after us, finally catching up at the Majestic.

Having our numbers swell to over a dozen at some stages led to some logistical problems in getting everyone finished their drinks and ready to move on at roughly the same time. This was especially problematical when not everyone was sitting together, but rather scattered about a bar engrossed in their own conversations.

Somehow the solution fell to me. I think I must have been watching *Kelly's Heroes* on TV a night or two before the Crawl. This has been one of my absolute favourite films since I first saw it, and my favourite character was Donald Sutherland's "Oddball".

For those who haven't seen the film, Oddball is a tank commander who is a hippy before hippies were invented. His tank is equipped to fire paint and play *The Ride Of The Valkyries* through a huge speaker ("frightens the hell out of the Germans, man..."). Oddball himself wears a leather flying helmet and frequently berates his exasperated mechanic Moriarty for his "negative waves, man".

Whenever the tank moves off at the head of Kelly's rag-tag bunch of bullion-heisting soldiers, Oddball leads the charge with a loud cry of, "YOOO-OOO!!!"

I think it seemed like a good idea at the time. Certainly everyone in the pub heard it. And they've been hearing it as a marshaling cry at just about every pub en route since. Funny how I'm usually hoarse the day after a Crawl...

In the Criterion Tavern we were joined by Budgie, celebrating his birthday with a Pub Crawl. Seemed apt. At the same time Buddy was looking like having some success in selling raffle tickets. The prize was Eric and Frog. The winner would get to pat Eric and keep Frog. The tape didn't make Judy's response to this clear – I'm not sure that she approved.

The York Hotel had gone trendy and was calling itself the New York.. While we apparently frightened off the bouncer, Frog and a friend of Toni's whose name eludes me were taken on a tour of the premises by someone described on tape as A Funny Little Man.

The Queen Street Mall only existed between Albert and Edward Streets at that time, but it was already seeing the demise of Her Majesty's. A large supply of Erics were collected and distributed. As Ern alluded to earlier, the establishment that later bore the name had absolutely none of the elegance and charm of the original. About the only thing in its favour (besides selling alcohol, obviously) was the wide staircase that became the setting for quite a number of 'group photographs' over the years.

It was somewhere around here that we had lunch, which for several of us was a scientific experiment. Someone had bought a tube of *Vita Glow Super B Complex Anti Stress Formula*. Each capsule contained three to four times the maximum daily recommended dose of Vitamin B. We had several each, and it didn't kill us.

Mid-afternoon we were weaving our way past a demolition site on Charlotte Street when it dawned on me what it was: the remains of the Arcadia Hotel. Security was pretty much non-existent as I wandered onto the demolition site amongst the heavy machinery to salvage several half-bricks for those who wanted them.

My own collection became depressingly large, with relics of departed pubs (mostly from Brisbane, with some Canberran and South Australian victims) sitting alongside fragments from other historic sites like Cloudland and Trades Hall. Eventually all but the original Eric became part of a feature wall in the garden of a house I sold in 2013.

As we tracked along George Street we discovered that the Zebra Motor Inn had undergone a name change and was now... the Bellevue Hotel! If that wasn't effrontery enough, it didn't even have a public bar!

Somehow, even without daylight saving it was still quite light as we staggered back across Victoria Bridge on our way homewards. Little groups within the group travelled with arms around each other's waists. Oh sure, it was as much to avoid falling over as anything else, but I look at the photo of us crossing the bridge, and I see the bonding and sharing of delight in each other's company that has kept us reassembling for Eric every year since.

.o0o.

5 1984 – A SMALL CROWD, BUT A HAPPY ONE

Perhaps it was the weather – I seem to recall it was even more than usually hot – but on the 1st of December 1984 there were only six of us (and a half-a-brick) who fronted up to the bar at the City View for the 10 o'clock start. The Two Michaels joined Eric and I, with Niall, Ian McLeod, and Karen Reid very determined not to be The Token Sheila.

The City View overlooked Albert Park on Leichhardt Street. It held memories of my schooldays, slipping in for furtive drinks on the way back from Grammar (or trying to – school uniforms were pretty obvious, and paid attention to by at least some bar staff). It was an interesting pub, with the outside done in a white stucco, and arched windows that always made me think of haciendas.

There was something cooling about that exterior, which contrasted with the vaguely gloomy interior. It was here I ate my first garlic brains, although not on a Pub Crawl, fortunately. Later the spot was occupied by a far more salubrious establishment – the Grand Chancellor Hotel in its multi-storey upstairs/upmarket guise, and down below, confusingly, the Spring Hill Tavern.

We took it in turns to take photographs of our little band as we worked our way into town. My own favourite is one that Michael Pegg took outside the Victory. We're slumped on the footpath in various states of disarray, recognizable but quite out of focus. What *is* clearly visible is the parking meter in front of us, displaying the appropriate message EXPIRED.

For many years there had been a public bar on Ann Street, the back door of which opened onto Platform 1 of Central Station. We'd always been keen to include it on a Crawl – it was listed in '79 – but Queensland Rail had apparently made a decision a while earlier that there weren't enough commuters to justify opening on Saturdays. With the extensive remodeling of the station we had the opportunity to remedy things somewhat as the Whistlestop Bar opened. Never big but usually fun, this busy little bar in the middle of the station complex became a regular Crawl venue, even after Fihelly's Arms opened in the ols Ann Street premises.

The top end of Queen Street still hadn't yet become part of the Queen Street Mall, and the York Hotel was battling to retain its snazzy existence as the New York. It had a public bar reminiscent of a long yellow tunnel with a big plain glass picture window looking out onto Queen Street. An ageing argumentative drunk took exception to Karen's presence amongst us, accusing her of being "unladylike".

Michael Pegg attempted to step in to defend her honour (brave considering he was outweighed by a factor of about 3:1). That wasn't necessary though, as Karen defended herself by putting the complainer in his place with a stream of invective that *a.* pinned him back to his stool, and *b.* was decidedly not ladylike.

Further along, in the Mall proper, a young constable approached me expressing grave concern that the half-brick I was carrying was some sort of concealable weapon. He was apparently worried that I was intending to throw Eric through a window, or at someone, or something of that nature. I started having flashbacks to 1979 and wondered where was Ern when I needed him. Or Barbara and her mother.

Karen rushed up to the officer and quickly tried to explain Eric's history. "He could no more throw Eric at someone than he could assault them with his own child. If he had one. He has the brick instead. But it's like a child to him…"

Another bemused policeman. Another "Be on your way – I don't want to see you again". Despite the fearsome reputation of the Queensland police – a reputation they'd done much to deserve over the years – Eric continued to lead a charmed life.

My attire that year turned out to be the precursor of a continuing tradition. I wore a t-shirt with a hand-drawn likeness of Eric and the words 1984 Eric The Half-A-Brick Annual Testimonial Pub Crawl. It inspired a succession of Crawl t-shirts in subsequent years.

I still have that shirt, and all its successors. I'd like to say I still fit into it, but after all these years I wouldn't be fooling anyone, would I? Would you believe, it shrank?

.o0o.

6 1985 – INCREASING VISIBILITY

This was the year of the first Official t-shirts. A simple design, based on my hand-drawn effort of '84, printed in traditional Queensland maroon on white. We were starting to look like an organized event. Maybe we were subconsciously inspired by it being the centenary of the Belle Vue's construction.

I'd spent a disturbing part of the year off work due to a neck injury sustained in a car accident. (Disturbing because of the pain and some drug side-effects – I wasn't disturbed by being off work.) To alleviate my boredom at one stage while planning the '85 Eric I sent an invitation and covering note to Brisbane's various newspapers.

At that time the residents of Brisbane were still served by a choice of local newspapers. Monday to Saturday there was the Courier-Mail in the morning, and the Telegraph in the afternoon, then there was either or both of the Sunday Mail and the Sunday Sun.

I didn't actually hear anything back beforehand – I may even have forgotten that I'd made the effort – but it turned out we *had* been noticed.

One worthwhile regular read in the Tele was Mike O'Connor's *Eye Q* column. This was a one or two page feature wherein Mike would chat about anything that took his fancy, serious or otherwise. It was sometimes controversial, sometimes newsy, and often funny.

Mike had received the Eric invitation, and about a week after the November 9 event apologised for his non-attendance with a feature *In memory of the Pub Crawl.*

After describing our event, Mike waxed reminiscent about pub crawls of his journalistic younger days (I didn't, and still don't think he was that old!). At the end of the column he suggested he'd be a more likely starter were we to provide him with a wheelchair, and someone to push it from pub to pub.

He also mentioned that he looked forward to reading "the steward's report". That thought was duly filed away...

The six starters from the year before were joined by Michael Perisic's girlfriend Debbie, Toni, Buddy returning after a year off, '79 alumnus Cleo and his girlfriend Jo, slightly eccentric English cartoonist Alan Smith, and thereafter stalwart Matt Taylor. Budgie sent his apologies, his brother Rob having just been injured in a car accident, he had other priorities to deal with.

As the number of inner city pubs continued to decline, we realised that to maintain a challenging itinerary we'd have to look further afield. That meant starting down in Fortitude Valley and being a bit creative with our route, which was:

Brunswick	Empire	Royal George
Prince Consort	Orient	National
Story Bridge	Port Office	Embassy
Carlton	Treasury	Lennons
Criterion	George St. Station (*a temporary name for the City Plaza Tavern*)	
	Crest	Wintergarden
Rosies	Whistlestop	Brisbane
St. Paul's	Sportsman	Spring Hill
City View	Normanby.	

Number 7 on that list was the start of what became a popular tradition: the ferry rides to and from the Story Bridge. There have been plenty of ferry drivers since that day who've had to endure our free-for-all versions of singing. I wish I could recall with certainty, but it seems likely that 1985 saw the first rendition of *Gilligan's Island*, the TV theme that became something like our theme.

It was at the National that we had our other brush with the media. The Sun had sent a photographer to "catch up with us". They could have saved travel time for the poor sod if they'd sent him to meet us at the Empire earlier, seeing as how that was right next door to the Sunday Sun Building!

Several happy group shots were taken outside the Nash, some in the doorway and some with the Story Bridge in the background looking suitably iconic.

The Sun never did print the story or photos (although we did get copies of them). We weren't told why, either. One thought was that they didn't want to be seen to encourage excessive drinking. Another was that Jo's decision to wear a school uniform may have cast doubts about the legal drinking age of all the participants.

It's curious to reflect that not only is the National Hotel now long gone, so too are the Sunday Sun and the Telegraph.

Already gone by this Crawl was the dear old Grosvenor, with its distinctive long public bar formed of a single seamless sheet of milled Scandinavian stainless steel – I think the only one of its type in Australia. I never did buy a Big Mac there.

At day's end Michael, Karen, Alan and I were making our merry way home from the Normanby to the flat Helen and I had in Red Hill. The weather, which had held out for us during the duration of the Crawl, now turned wet.

We were well past caring though, and continued regardless. In fact, it was enough to provoke some bad Gene Kelly impressions as we went *Singin' In The Rain*.

Unfortunately, as a dancer Michael Pegg was a brilliant footballer. Half a block from home he fell off the footpath. "Ow. My ankle's hurt." Luckily Mike's not very heavy, even when he's wringing wet, so it wasn't too difficult to carry him the rest of the way to the flat.

I know my sports medicine: "We'll put ice on it." Helen patiently pointed out that we didn't have any. No problem. Only a few days earlier I'd read how a great cold pack for treating soft tissue injuries could be made from a packet of frozen peas. These were cold, and would mould easily to the shape of the injured body part.

"We haven't got any frozen peas," replies Helen.

Stubbornly I checked the freezer for myself, and was able to apply some drunk's lateral thinking.

And so it was that Michael woke up next morning with a sad and soggy packet of now-thawed broccoli tied to his foot...

.oOo.

7 1986 – GETTING OFFICIAL

I think the blame can be laid at the feet of Mike O'Connor. At the end of his 1985 column he'd mentioned a desire to read a "steward's report", and over a bottle or two of wine one night I think Helen, Judy and I extrapolated from there.

A fresh interest in heraldry prompted Judy's suggestion that we devise an official crest to adorn t-shirts in that and subsequent years. Some people were still trying to squeeze into their old 'crested' shirts more than ten years later...

Eric is of course centred on the shield, against a background of a setting sun and a pile of rubble, symbolizing the demise of the Belle Vue. The shield is actually a beer glass complete with handle and foamy head, and is leaning to one side, denoting too many drinks. It balances on a field of the odd jigsaw-shaped bricks with which much of Brisbane's CBD footpaths had recently been paved. Also standing on the 'footpath' is the little cartoon brick drawn by Mac Vines for Mike's 1985 column, holding a placard that said, 'As seen in the Telegraph'. A couple of inebriated-looking cherubs held aloft the banner.

Looking back, I'm actually quite proud of it. It may well yet be revived for a future t-shirt.

The crest wasn't the only move towards 'organizing' the event more efficiently. Starting from Mike's idea of a steward's report, we devised a team of Officials: Helen as Chief Steward, Renoir as Logistics Commander, and Judy as Logistics Support. I suspect Helen got the steward's job on the grounds that we thought she'd be more sober and thus more literate than I would be. Not unreasonable.

'86 was to be the first year when Awards were really recognized.

Worst injury sustained on the Crawl would receive the Frozen Broccoli Award in honour of the creative first aid job done on Michael Pegg's ankle in 1985.

I can't recall what inspired the thought that a Golden Bladder Award (for greatest holding capacity, not greatest frequency of relief) was a good idea. It was, however, keenly contested for several years before age, good sense and self-preservation prevailed.

This year also saw the first appearance of the Official Brick Carrier's Nose – a red plastic clown nose to be worn by whoever was carrying Eric at the time. Another silly innovation that enjoyed remarkable longevity until quite reasonable sensitivities about germ transferal won out.

A number of auspicious debuts were made. Mark (Lurch) Moore made the first of many appearances. Later years' photographs provide a pictorial history of the growth of his kids Sophie and Jack, first brought along to wave goodbye to their Dear Ol' Dad and eventually being old enough to be legal participants in their own right.

Adam Cretier came down from Toowoomba with Lurch and drank nothing but Coke, a tradition he carried on into the next millennium.

Marc Hunter became a regular, and his brothers Wayne and Brad later added some memorable moments. It was also the debut of Neale Dewar, who went on to grace the RAF and regularly celebrate traditional English Real Ale. Nowadays he's in Belgium and is supporting the excellent local brewing industry there.

There were major travellers. Michael Pegg and Karen Reid journeyed up from Melbourne, Buddy Doyle over from W.A., and Matt Taylor down from Biloela resplendent in a purple-dyed and hand-painted version of the official t-shirt.

Toni's partner Carmel bravely turned up on crutches, and proceeded to survive more of the Crawl than a few more able-bodied participants.

Mike O'Connor was again invited, and as he'd alluded to previously, we offered to provide a wheelchair pusher. Although he didn't attend, in generous response we got a two page feature article headed *Boozathon '86* – coverage we were quite chuffed with! This year's article, published about a fortnight before the Crawl, focused more on our event than Mike's own recollections of misspent youth. It led to a few new and unfamiliar faces joining us at the Normanby at 10 o'clock on December 13.

The Steward's Report was in the end, I think, a joint effort between Helen's notes and my scribblings. It went like this:

1. NORMANBY Finally finished first round and departed by 10:30. 32 people, which number did **not** include well-known journalist and Pub Crawl enthusiast M. O'Connor.
2. CITY VIEW First casualty of the day – Tina's pants – were repaired by the Chief Steward's judicious application of sticky tape. Lyn & Bruce Barry arrived.
3. SPRING HILL Public Bar too small to hold the entire assemblage so the management (bravely) suggested we use the Private Bar. Buddy issued a formal challenge to the Logistics Commander – current holder of the Golden Bladder, as did Toni, Alan and Periscope. Jon Nicholls gave a copy of the itinerary to a barmaid he was trying to chat up in the hope of seeing her again later. Dawn and Steve the first to leave. Remember the Bobsey Twins! A souvenir – a battered copy of Roy Orbison's *The Big O*, was rescued from the middle of Leichhardt Street.
4. SPORTSMAN The coldest beer so far! Marc spotted drinking only a 5oz beer. Leon the Klingon arrived just as we departed.
5. ALLIANCE Our first Carlton pub for some years, but there's now a majority of spirit drinkers, and pub numbers are dwindling, so... Matthew became first candidate for the Frozen Broccoli Award.
6. ST PAULS Midday, overrunning the beer garden and soaking up the sun (and the alcohol). Running behind time!
7. BRISBANE The newest hobby: hat swapping. Gary Thwaites falls down the stairs and becomes a contender for the Frozen Broc.
8. WHISTLESTOP Buddy voted this the best gin so far. Everyone did their best to ignore the Logistics Commander headbutting ice-cubes into his glass.

9. CAPITOL Not for the acrophobic! Horrible lifts not for the claustrophobic, either. Bruce's creative photography from great heights.
10. ROSIES Phone calls from Logistics Support to Defence to drum up further support (we hoped). Ewan, veteran of the 79 inaugural Crawl bid us farewell. His presence had been much appreciated..
11. HER MAJESTY'S Toni enters the running for the Frozen Broc Award. This bar sold wine by the glass, but the Chief Steward regarded $3 for a Wolf Blass Yellow Label as unreasonable. Budgie and Jo arrived. Toni accidentally (?) threw a jug of cold water over Iain Moore's lap.
12. WINTERGARDEN Some delays caused by various people's insistence on consuming McPlastics etc.
13. EMBASSY James Townley – the youngest Crawler of '86, calls it a day. Not bad for a 17-year-old vegetarian.
14. ORIENT A round of applause for Tina's tissue please! *(I have no idea what this means – Renoir)*
15. NATIONAL The taking on of Dutch courage before the perilous cross river ferry ride. Said ride was characterized by the loud singing of sea shanties, and an Asian mother and her three children cowering bemusedly in a corner.
16. STORY BRIDGE Made to feel very welcome when this pub sent a minibus to the ferry terminal to collect us, then presented all participants with a souvenir keyring. Carlton Light Ale – inappropriate, but it's the thought that counts. A bit of a delay because the Chief Steward wanted to eat a roast turkey sandwich with gherkin relish. Actually, other people wanted to eat too, it being about 4:30. Lurch became a contender for the Frozen Broccoli with a spectacular flight along the footpath. Leon declared a "half-assed fruit" for breaking *The Big O*. Jon bears testimony that the Chief Steward carried Eric and wore the Official Ceremonial Nose on the next leg of the Crawl.
17. PORT OFFICE Amazing! This time we didn't get asked to leave the Public Bar or the beer garden, where some fine music was being played. Wendy Moore finally called it quits after a brave effort.
18. VICTORY Matt 'Granny' Townsend accosted two strangers with the line "You can't come in here with collared shirts" – one of them growled.

19. EXCHANGE Another welcoming pub, who provided not free food as expected, but free jugs of beer! The Logistics Commander climbed onto the bar to deliver a moving "thank you" speech. Lurch was observed standing transfixed in front of the TV giggling at Tweety Pie cartoons and making noises in time with the sound effects.
20. TREASURY Gary pointed out that he was as pissed as a fart three pubs ago.
21. LENNONS Jon declared that he was out of the running for the Golden Bladder, but that "he'd only been twice".
22. CRITERION En route, Eric was struck by a Volvo and slightly chipped. So too was Gary, who was carrying him at the time. Other occupants of the bar were woken by a birthday cheer for Iain.
23. PLAZA Rude service led to suggestions that this pub be deleted from next year's list.
24. CREST Marc becomes the latest Broccoli contender, falling off the footpath. Kelly Dixon declared an Attendant Pisshead. The Chief Steward was sung at. (Most alarming!)
25. MAJESTIC The bar was cleared of non-Crawlers by a Community Singalong. The Chief Steward prompted by 'Waterfront' Joe McLaughlin to carry Eric and wear the Official Nose to the Trans.
26. TRANSCONTINENTAL Closed! A sad finish, although some Crawlers returned to the Normanby to kick on. Others were poured into taxis, while others were seen standing yelling inanities on the footpath outside the Governor's residence in the late evening.

The GOLDEN BLADDER AWARD was eventually tied between Buddy Doyle and the Logistics Commander, both of whom completed the entire official course un-unemcumbered.

 Some notes on the above. The Bobsey Twins (3) was a name Toni coined for the Toowoomba contingent of Adam and Lurch. Quite without planning it, they'd both turned up dressed in matching canary yellow shirts over their Pub Crawl tees.

 Spirit drinking (5) was superseding beer as we recognized that, lovely as the amber fluid may be, twenty-something inputs meant a gas build-up to leave one waddling like an ambulatory blimp.

The Capitol (11) was a sadly short-lived bar with one of the best locations in town. It was on the roof of the old Canberra Hotel – the Temperance League Headquarters on the corner of Edward and Ann! Bruce Barry took a drunk's risk leaning wa-a-ay out over a guard rail to get a dizzying photograph of the Crawlers on Ann Street far below. On that site opposite the Salvo's (later backpackers') People's Palace, there's now just another glass-and-steel business building.

We discovered the benefits of pre-warning some pubs (16 and 19). John Edwards and rugby league legend John Sattler – hosts at the Stock Exchange – got advance notice by virtue of running the pub opposite where I worked in Charlotte Street at the time. And the Story Bridge was a popular spot for Gary Thwaites and I to stop in for a quiet ale on the way home from work.

Their positive responses offset some of our fears that some pubs would make us unwelcome if advised of our planned arrival. Sadly there have been enough negatives (and enough demands for impossible foreknowledge of "what time we'd arrive, and how many?") to keep advance warnings the exception and not the rule.

Lurch was declared the winner of the Frozen Broccoli Award (16). His flight came about as he ran along the footpath to alert Marc and I to an attractive blonde in skimpy clothes pushbiking past us. He lost his footing and flew by, startlingly parallel to the ground calling, "Hey! Did you see her?" before landing in a heap.

There are rather unpleasant memories of blood trickling down his arm and dripping into a Cooper's Ale that was consumed anyway. Just added to the cloudiness, I suppose. The Award was really earned, though, because it took until the next morning for him to notice that his arm was actually sore, go to the hospital (a drive I probably shouldn't have made), and have his busted wrist put into a plaster cast.

.o0o.

8 1987 – ERIC IN ANOTHER STATE

For reasons not relevant to this book I left Queensland in January of 1987 to work in the head Office of Tax in our nation's capital – Canberra.

Eric himself had, of course, gone to stay in the ACT with me. (Helen hadn't but that's another story.)

There were some who feared that this would mean the end of the Annual Pub Crawl, but they underestimated the power of tradition! That, and the fact that I was aware that a Crawl was a great opportunity to catch up with many people I hadn't seen since I'd gone south.

By September I'd already done the drive 'home' – it still felt like that – several times. Enough to know that it was a trip better made with company. Luckily, while in Canberra I'd met up with a number of people who shared some of my interests, most particularly drinking.

Eric's and my travelling companions were Ross (Rosco) Kelly, Joe Ziliotto and Karl Johnston. I rather thought I'd enthusiastically invited a number of my best mates to share an important bonding experience with me. Well, something like that. Karl remembers his invitation somewhat differently.

Happy Hour after work. I'd never spoken to this guy before, and his first words to me were, "Pub Crawl. You coming?"

Visions of a few quiet drinks in a few quiet bars, then strolling home to bed. Then other visions of a travelling riot, blind drunk and lost, a night in the city watchhouse. Slurred explanations to family and magistrate, apologies. "No, I don't think so. Thanks."

Famous last words.

We had never formally met, but I had seen him around at work, at the local pubs, at Happy Hours. He was noisy, colourful, relentlessly gregarious. Except with me. Until now. "Name's Eric." *(Of course, I meant the Pub Crawl's name, or the half-a-brick's...)*

And so we talked. We identified a shared thirst for beer, and an enthusiasm for gin and tonic. An appreciation of notes written and sung, of stories observed and invented and shared.

He told me about The Brick. History, community, a disdain for false authority and those who take it seriously, and flipping great buckets of booze. "Okay. When and where?"

There is an old illustration of gold miners drinking and dancing. One man dances, one knee up and a curved arm raised, bearded face looking downward as though concentrating on performing his Australian Irish jig. When I looked at this bloke, I saw the old miner.

"Brisbane. Saturday. I'm driving."

Hmm. Not the local, then.

No, not local at all. Karl, Ross, Joe and I piled into Bernadette, my trusty Commodore, and headed north. The trip up the Newell Highway was fairly uneventful, though it went a long way towards furthering friendships as we got to know each other better. Karl has a few specific memories:

Breakfast in a Ronald's on the Gilded Coast. Preparatory drinks and lunch:
    A food hall
    Rock'n'roll dancers, couples, skirts akimbo
    A guy in pseudo military garb, striding around the perimeter, looking suspicious and pilfering food from the counter.

Caravan park booked by Renoir. "Your hair is too long, you can't stay here, you'll upset the residents." And so this is Queensland.

"Males hair must be off the ears and the neck," we were told. Poor old conservative Rosco was mortified to learn he looked too disreputable for the lawn bowling community who comprised most of the park's permanent residents. (The further irony, of course, is that not long after this Rosco, Karl and I were all playing competitive lawn bowls.) At least we got our deposit back.

Irritated and not a little embarrassed, I led the troops to a friendly bar (the Normanby), where the barman recommended we try the backpackers' accommodation 'down the road'. We duly traipsed down Petrie Terrace to the *Paddington Barracks*. This was a fine old pub going through one of its many changes of identity.

I'd always known it as the Prince Alfred, and after its foray into the lucrative hostel trade it was seriously trendified (like much of the surrounding area) and became the Hotel LA.

At $7 each per night including breakfast, we couldn't fault it for value. Karl recalls bunk beds, and newspapers: no titties on page 3. Damn, what a letdown, it seemed like a "titties on page 3" kind of place.

The four of us taxied over to the Brekky Creek for a pre-Crawl dinner of steak and XXXX 'off the wood', a legendary experience I was keen to share. Sadly, despite invitations none of the local Crawlers turned up to join us. Helen later apologised and explained her Cortina had a flat battery – I never did like that car. Never mind, the four of us had fun.

As we did the next day – September 12 – as Eric had his first Crawl as an interstater.

After another Normanby Hotel start we made our way downhill through the Spring Hill Fair.

At a stall there Brad Hunter bought a cheap little kaleidoscope, possibly thinking that a Pub Crawl wouldn't distort his vision enough. He christened his new toy the Brain Scanner, and proceeded to peer through it into as many earholes as possible as the day progressed.

This was a harmless pursuit that didn't annoy anyone too greatly, except for one barman in the Embassy who emphatically *didn't* want his brain scanned, and chased Brad away with a broom... This was after Brad had made his entrance there doing his bizarre impression of a Romanian gymnast. And then tried to help speed up service by reaching over the bar to pour his own beer.

The beer garden at St. Paul's Tavern was briefly converted into Tina's School of Creative Hairdressing. The then Mrs. Thwaites amused herself and others by plaiting the locks of Jack Dempsey, yours truly, and I think a few others.

Budgie was only a fleeting visitor, unfortunately, but he did bring a gift. We now had a Golden Bladder Award trophy – a two litre specimen bottle. It had never been used, and despite the implicit challenge we never did see if a trophy winner could fill it at the end of a Crawl. The first winner to actually receive the trophy was Buddy Doyle, taking the honours in what was becoming a two-man continuing saga for him and me.

I'll hand back to Karl for his recollections of his first Eric:
I took my scungy jacket to the Eric – first words anyone spoke to me: "you won't need that." Renoir's ex-wife offered to carry spare bags and jackets.
She lost mine somewhere, with tears and self-recrimination.
I showed her that I still had all my possessions – keys, wallet, etc. It didn't help.

By Crawl's end the survivors were Toni, Jack, Niall, Toni's brother Kieran, Brad, and the Canberra contingent (who, as Karl pointed out, comprised 2 from Adelaide, a Hobartian, and a Brisbanite from Scotland). Fiona was throwing a party that night, but Joe and I were the only Canberrans with the strength left to attend. A pity, because Katie was there and she'd definitely caught Rosco's eye enough to be fondly remembered long after.

Sunday was of course a recovery day. The afternoon was spent drinking and listening to a rockabilly band called the Convertibles in the beer garden at St. Paul's. Now <u>there</u> was a place to while away a sunny afternoon. Another one gone…

The drive home on Monday turned memorable for the wrong reasons. Late at night, travelling from Gunnedah, about 40 kms out from Coonabarabran, Rosco at the wheel. We're near the crest of a hill. Trees on our left, bloody big semi-trailer approaching on the right. Kangaroo hops out in front of us. What to hit? What to hit?

Bye bye, Skippy. Good choice, Rosco. He was upset. The rest of us weren't – we were alive. And in a lot better shape than the radiator on poor old Bernadette The Commodore. **Radiator smashed, blood shit and gore** is Karl's memory.

The car was nursed the rest of the way to Coonabarabran and deposited at an NRMA garage. Good thing I'd renewed my RACQ membership only that morning! We managed to get a couple of rooms at the Imperial Hotel, and watched a motorcycle Grand Prix over a few calming ales. Karl recalls it as Wayne Gardner winning world championship – first I'd ever heard of him.

We spent a year in Coona next day, waiting for Bernadette to be made mobile again. Did a local Pub Crawl – it didn't take long, with only the Imperial, Royal and Coonabarabran Hotels and the Bowling Club to visit. I annoyed a Senior Citizen by winning a small jackpot on a poker machine that "was <u>her</u> machine!" It didn't help when I pointed out that she'd left the machine to go and play bingo – apparently I should have known it was <u>always</u> reserved for her…

Not surprisingly, it was good to see Coona receding in the rear view mirror. We were a day late returning to work, having gotten in to Canberra after midnight Wednesday morning. Luckily we had photos of the car damage, and receipts, to convince people that our late return was *not* hangover related!

And Bernadette was the first and only car to receive the Frozen Broccoli Award.

.o0o.

9 1988 – EKSHPO? WHAT EKSHPO?

I should admit up front that I bore a grudge against Brisbane's Expo '88. In fact, a couple of them.

On a personal front, it had cost Helen and I a flat we really liked. The Villa in Highgate Hill (referred to in the chapter on 1983) overlooked the Expo site, and once the event was announced our weekly rent leapt, as I recall by about 200%.

Further, a large percentage of my work in the mid-80s was with businesses in the South Brisbane/West End area, and I watched far too many driven to closure to 'clear the site'. Family businesses which had existed in the same spot for generations, surviving on 'passing trade', were paid inadequate compensation as they were relocated to backblocks in far corners of West End where even the locals seldom drove by.

The final straw was the closure of the View World Hotel, formerly the Princess. This was home to what had been arguably the best bottle shop in Brisbane, and was my regular working hours watering hole. What mystified me then, and still does, is that this fine old pub (still in good nick despite its age) was tagged for demolition by the same geniuses who decided to sink millions into the refurbishment of the derelict Sip Inn at the other end of Southbank. Historic link with the old Brisbane wharves as it may have been, it had already been long closed and condemned as unsafe. It looked like one good sneeze would bring much of it crashing down.

There's an old legend that the Ship Inn's first owner – a blackbirding rogue named Captain "Bully" Hayes – buried a cache of ill-gotten treasure under the pub, and that treasure has never been found. A cynic suggested to me that the Ship wasn't demolished because the government didn't want any workmen to stumble on any buried treasure on *their* property. All I'll say is that it's a good story.

Having said all that, yes, I did visit the Expo with Gill on a visit back to Brisbane, and yes I did enjoy it (although that was as much or more due to the company). What's more, yes I admit the post-Expo development of Southbank has been extremely impressive and I've since spent a lot of good times there – not just on Pub Crawls.

But during the planning stages of the 88 Eric all of that was in the future, and my prevailing mood was cynicism. This was compounded by the decision to have the Expo mascot designed by the Disney Corporation. I'm still inclined to believe the rumour that they just recoloured a Donald Duck costume and changed the outfit from a pseudo sailor's suit to a pseudo Digger's uniform.

The blue-billed platypus became the star of the year's t-shirt – cross-eyed drunk, slumped in front of a bar on which sat Eric, and slurring the words "Ekshpo? What Ekshpo?". It was then and still remains one of my favourite Pub Crawl t-shirts.

While I was still officially a Canberran, the majority of my time was being spent in Adelaide, and it was from there that Eric and I travelled for the 88 Crawl. We drove up via Canberra in faithful old Bernadette, and en route collected Karl, who had gotten the Eric bug. An overnight drive on Thursday brought us to our temporary home: the hostel that was once the Coronation Hotel.

One thing I recall is that there were insufficient showers for the numbers there, so we traipsed across the river to use the travellers' facilities at the Transit Centre.

Karl relates a story of the trip up that my memory had blotted out.

Mars was at its closest conjunction for x hundred years, bright (as bright as Mars gets).
>   Me: "It's bright, red."
>   Renoir: "I can't see red, but I can see it's bright."
>   Car (approaching fast from other side of crest): "Zoom."
>   Both: "gulp…"
>   We pay attention to the road for a while.

Nonetheless, we all made it in one piece, and on September 24 assembled with our fellow friends of Eric back at the Transit Centre. There were plenty of familiar faces and some new ones, including Richard (Dirk) Hartog – former housemate of Rhys, Robbo, Cleo, Helen and I (now *there* was a group household!) – and a foursome of comparative youngsters named Greg, Simon, Scotty and Roscoe. How they came to join us, and whatever happened to them, I don't know. But they fitted right in.

For reasons now lost in the obscurity of time, I kept something headed as an (Unofficial) Steward's Report. It may have been an unofficial report, or I may have been an unofficial steward…

1. TRANSIT CENTRE By 10:00 there was already a substantial queue forming at the door of the Queenslander Bar. Within 30 minutes the numbers had grown to about 30 Crawlers
2. TRANSCONTINENTAL The two survivors of the Crawl of '79 *(Ern and Renoir)* shell out $15 for a jug of gin and tonic. Old habits may die hard, but old drunks die harder! Kronk *(Iain Moore)* bids a too-soon farewell, having had less than a day's notice of the event.
3. MAJESTIC Greg, Rhys and Renoir officially nominate for the Golden Bladder Award, vacated by Buddy who couldn't get down from PNG this year. Recent poor health causes Ern to withdraw early.
4. CITY PLAZA Lurch and Matthew find a man named Jack Wood who has an original oil painting of the Belle Vue. Jon is seen to chat up a bird, then let her walk away with her mates. He later denies this.
5. CRITERION En route, the populace of Brisbane is warned that "BRAD WORKS AT FOSSEY'S!!" In the bar, Norman declares himself (and is declared) a homosexual. Matt Granny Townsend has numerous wet fingers stuck in his ear – a tradition here. Complaints made about what tastes like Guinness cordial.
6. TREASURY Jon caught ordering Coke. Karl asked by yhe barmaid, "Are we all Americans?" Brad falls in lust with the picture on the condom vending machine. Marc, Rhys, Dirk, Frog, Karl and Renoir all file in to the Men's to see if they agree.

7   MYERS An unexpected bonus found by Marty. A jukebox featuring Easybeats, Louis Armstrong, old Rolling Stones and Queen – all sung along with. A barman who, after some initial intimidation at our numbers, laid on a jug or two. Brad briefly attempts to help behind the bar, but is sternly Frogged.

8   LENNONS Asked to leave because of our attire. Told that there <u>was</u> no Public Bar as it was being 'renovated'. There's supposed to be a law about that, isn't there?

9   CREST En route some tourists are helped with their holiday snaps. Coopers available at last! Marc: "They've got Guinness!" Renoir: "Is it okay?" Marc (sculling pint): "Yep." Olympic watching by many – some black guy beat some other black guy named Lewis.

10 WHISTLESTOP Simon buys a Coke but is then forced to scull a beer. Spirits noted as seeming stronger here. Norman Thomas debagged, regarded as noteworthy by few, least of all Denise, heard to remark, "Such a fuss over a little thing."

11 ROSIES Australia beat Pakistan 4-0 in hockey. So? Frog expresses dissatisfaction at Brad for dancing on the furniture. Greg's bladder cracks.

12 HER MAJESTY'S Someone notices "the VFL's on" – Renoir, Marty and several others disappear to the next-door bar, leaving the rest to enjoy (?) the singer.

13 WINTERGARDEN The barmaid is (eventually) cajoled into letting Lurch change TV channels. Hawthorn lead 28-11 at quarter time. The last challengers have cracked and Renoir regains the Golden Bladder Award. Phew.

14 EMBASSY Renoir celebrates with $5 worth of Onion Rings. Considerable drama with the alleged theft of a bar towel which Lurch then found in the Men's. Well, he's a hero to <u>somebody</u> anyway. Whatever happened to Marc?

15 VICTORY Young Roscoe arrested <u>in</u> the bar for "abusive language". *(Perhaps remarkably, this remains the only arrest during an Eric.)* Premiers may change but it seems coppers never will. Greg, Simon and Scotty leave to secure his release from the watch-house.

16 STOCK EXCHANGE Told to "keep it down or we'll be asked to leave". So we kept it down and left after Jill Smith-Moore arrived with The Photo Album.

17 PORT OFFICE Didn't get thrown out *again* this year – they must be getting used to us. Excellent band, whatever they were playing.

FERRY – which almost wouldn't take us. Brad and Renoir fail to acquire rowboats. Raucous sea shanties as usual.

18 STORY BRIDGE Hawthorn win the VFL. Renoir goes a bit silly and has a pie fight with Norman. Jim restores calm by buying Renoir a liqueur mead.

FERRY – upon the roof of which Brad surfs across the river.

19 ORIENT Closed. Again. "Oh, we shut at 5. There's no business after that." THIS is a tourist capital?!?

20 BRISBANE Karl is served a gin and tonic that is patently not a gin and tonic. Only the staff fail to recognize this.

21 ALLIANCE Only Karl, Lurch and Renoir appear here next as scheduled. The rest have stopped across the road as it was on the way. Most friendly barman – Renoir spills a straight gin (putz!) and has it cheerfully replaced free!

22 ST. PAUL'S The three in the Ekshpo t-shirts trade places with the other survivors (Niall, Michael, Frog, Brad, Jon, Russ, Matthew, Rhys and Pete). The last Officially Listed pub on the Crawl. Various farewells.

23 SPORTSMAN Only Karl, Lurch, Niall, Rhys, Renoir and Pete remain. Vague blithering at a band of punks who may have been wondering if this is what *they'll* be like when they're this old.

24 SPRING HILL Video jukebox. Propped against a wall, not very successfully watching a game of pool being played. Lurch and Niall let discretion be the better part of valour.

25 CITY VIEW A quiet conclusion, the four survivors not being up to much else. Last drinks, last farewells, and it's see you again next year for another mobile party!

Brad indulged in a bit of racial pot-stirring in the Crest. I've decided not to preserve the details, but it was a particularly brave/stupid thing to do as the bar was full of American gentlemen of colour at the time, all of whom were considerably bigger than him. Luckily they were mostly too engrossed in the race to notice him, and the few who did took one look and decided he wasn't worth the trouble.

Marc has some less-than-clear recollections of whatever happened to him (14 above). As he tells it, he remembers, "escaping from Denise and Tracey in the Mall, near the Wintergarden". His next conscious recollection is of being in the Story Bridge Hotel, and having a "moment of clarity" halfway through a schooner of Coopers. He put down the glass and called a taxi. The brain cells black out again then, until a mental picture forms of knocking on the door of Jenny's place.

The theory goes that he'd forgotten his own (admittedly quite new) address, but had that of his girlfriend on a piece of paper in his pocket. He shoved that at the cabbie, burbling, "Take me here."

Popular mythology has it that Marc woke up the next morning engaged, that having been a condition of his being allowed in. Indeed, he was later considered for the Frozen Broccoli on the basis of having lost his singularity. Marc and Jenny both, however, deny this element of the story.

Karl and I spent the Sunday recovering on the Gold Coast, staying at a Backpackers that had quite a good little bar of its own.

On the Monday we went back into Brisbane to collect photos and do a bit of touristing. We visited a dingy little something called Wilderness Walk on the corner of Creek and Adelaide Streets. I dimly remember glass cases in a basement room, and my observation at the time was, "Oh look – stuffed dead things."

Later we called in on the Irish Club to visit a farewell function for Merv Russell. Merv was an ex-Navy officer who'd worked with me in Australia Post back in '79 – a charming, dignified man who'd earned my friendship and respect despite our *very* different personalities.

Karl's recollections of Sunday and Monday go like this:
Sunday, afterwards, hungry
> Late dinner at a restaurant in Coolangatta *(the fine Rum Jungle)*
> Renoir too sleepy, eats a portion, then apologizes and farewells
> Me, caught short by sudden runs, runs to gents room
> Returns to empty table, cleared by efficient staff
> Goes to bed, still hungry.

Next afternoon, farewell drinks for Renoir's ex-co-worker
       Lite beer, not a good one for the road.
Cassettes – Frank Zappa "Mothers Of Prevention (European Version)", repeated numerous times
All nighter
We drove right under gigantic thunderheads
Heavy rain
       Very heavy rain
              Still heavier rain, poor visibility
       Getting passed by big trucks – either a better view or Benzedrine stupidity up there
Straight back to work next morning

After '87's run-in with the local wildlife I'd had a bull bar fitted to Bernadette (painted purple and stenciled as the Violet Crumple Bar).

The incredible visibility-destroying downpour started just as we passed through That Place again – Coona-bloody-barabran! Still, at least this time we made it home without accident!

.oOo.

10 88-89 THE SUPPLEMENT

There had been a few people who'd complained in September '88 that for various reasons they couldn't get to the Crawl. For their benefit it was decided to hold a once-only supplementary Crawl: 1988 revisited. I'm not protecting anyone's reputations when I say that I can't remember who the relevant people were – but I do know that it was observed that most of "them" (whoever they were) didn't turn up to the Supplementary Crawl on June 10, 1989 either!

Since it was 88 revisited, the same route was reprised. I even kept another Unofficial Steward's Report.

By now, Eric and I were officially domiciled in Adelaide, and it was from there that we drove north with my lady love Gill, and Richard Faulkner.

As well as working with us, Young Dick had become a key member of the theatre company that Gill and I were involved with at the time. We'd suggested that an Eric Testimonial was an excellent opportunity for him to be involved in some free form street theatre.

When we met up with other local Crawlers it was pointed out that Young Dick bore a more than passing resemblance to Wally Lewis. A pretty seriously out-of-shape Wally Lewis, admittedly, but a new nickname was born! I think it was at a later Crawl that Young Dick went so far as to buy himself a Broncos jersey to really underscore the resemblance.

I think we must have anticipated only a small turn-out, because I've noted somewhere that the 30-odd starters were rather more than expected. But at was also noted, "a splendid time was had by all!"

1. TRANSIT The return of a few familiar faces under unfamiliar hairstyles. Painting of Robbo's shirt. *(Just Divorced)* Where's Lurch? Brad's cartwheel – luckily it was Renoir's head he kicked.
2. TRANSCONTINENTAL Lurch finally arrives. So too did Neale and Sandra. Tina enters Frozen Broc – bruised shin when Brad landed on it. Helen drinking MILO.
3. MAJESTIC Police escort on the way here. Norman arrives, with his pants on.
4. CITY PLAZA Watching the baked bean wrestling on SKY. Official Joke from an old Digger at the bar: Why did the two nuns screw each other? So neither nun got none.
5. CRITERION No beer coasters for the Perisic collection! "Aussie Bicentennial Lucky Tickets" – no luck for Brad, Adam or Renoir. Eric spills Katie's drink.
6. TREASURY Niall and McClod point out "It's not real vodka, whatever it is!" Cold weather means McClod, Adam and Renoir are the only remaining Golden Bladder contenders, already. The condom machine is still here. Brad the Human Dart. Frog announces she's not talking to Brad as he's not a stimulating conversationalist. Alleged to have broken this vow 30 seconds later – denied. Rhys attempts to pull a condom over his own head.
7. BERTIES (formerly MYERS) Immediate raid on the jukebox. Spirit prices the best so far. McClod drops out of the Golden Bladder as Gill nominates in.
8. LENNONS "No entry" sez Rory. Brad's dive down the escalator rails. The decapitation of Jason Donovan. Marc's farewell.
9. CREST Ice-creams in King George Square – the man who didn't want his photo taken. Brad found the skinheads who used to live across the road. Adam took a photo of Frog's profile. Tina attacks Gary. (Ask *them* why.)
10. WHISTLESTOP We've lost Norman! He was last seen in the Men's at Lennons. Frog discovers the Instructions For Use on a condom packet. Dick finds Toblerone!
11. ROSIES Phone call to Toni – she may join us later. J. Donovan's face used as an ashtray.

12 HER MAJESTY'S Adam autographs *True Blue* and is recognized as a Media Superstar. Applause for John The Doorman.
13 WINTERGARDEN Vicki leaves for work. Gill finally retires so Renoir retains the Golden Bladder. We find Jim Walls. Adam: "Kremmen! You can't die! You're the only one who's seen the far side of Demis Roussos!"
14 EMBASSY At Hungry Jack's Gill was recognized by someone she went to High School with in Adelaide. Met April, the ex- of former Crawler Alan Smith. Wal went to the toilet and everyone looked at him cos "he had a condom thing on his head".
15 STOCK EXCHANGE Norman has been here for @ 2 hours waiting for us. Lurch came here straight from KFC and waited, waited. Judy (who John picked up a few pubs ago) picked up her boyfriend.
16 VICTORY Gary dozed off under the bar, but woke up again. Robbo's plait of red and blue makes him "look like a tampon" according to someone.
17 PORT OFFICE Robbo ill. Public bar closed due to six strippers.
18 STORY BRIDGE Brad, Frog, Joe, Helen and Jon leave after ferry. Mark watching the races. Marc phoned and can't make it. Bye bye Rob. Niall exited on one side of the river, Katie, Debbie, McClod and Felicity on the other side.
19 ORIENT Open!! A live band in the bar next door. Lurch rapt in the China Crisis. Can you get AIDS from a plastic nose?
20 BRISBANE Survivors: Wal, Gill, Tina, Rhys, Lurch, Fiona, Matt, Gary, John, Judy, Adam, Renoir. Tina's valiant effort to do 'the Call'.
21 ST PAULS Jill finally arrived. Nothing else memorable happened. Just about *everyone* gives Eric a drink.
22 ALLIANCE Renoir, in Arsenal hat, gets accosted by a Manchester United fan.
23 SPORTSMAN Renoir with ice up his nose, scrummed into a wall. It's all Wal's fault, and Adam's too. Holy Roman noses Batman. *Hey Hey* Red Faces – lots of applause for the guy with the mobile eyebrows.
24 SPRING HILL Adam listening to Sweet records. A "bloody Pom" buttonholed Englishman Gary. Judy and Peter playing pool.

> 25 INTERNATIONAL Since the City View had been knocked down since we finished there last year, Rhys and Renoir battled to acquire an Eric from the remains. Adam has been on three Crawls and had <u>no</u> alcohol to drink. Last drinks: Rhys, Gill, Renoir, Wal, Tina, Gary, Lurch, Jill, Matt, Fiona, Adam.

I should point out that the police escort (3) didn't *know* that's what they were. The photos make it pretty clear that they were just walking along George Street quite oblivious to the thirty or so Crawlers trooping along behind them. I suspect they did wonder why I dashed past them, turned and took their picture.

Somewhere along the upper Queen Street Mall we acquired a life sized cutout of Jason Donovan (8) – I've no idea how or who was responsible. As the notes indicate, this particular souvenir of the then-fresh-faced young *Neighbours* heart throb was on the wrong end of increasing indignities as the day wore on.

I think it was the April edition of the bloke's magazine *True Blue* (12) that ran a feature on Queensland's loose firearm laws. Headed "Last Of The Gun Nuts" it had photos of, and interviews with, locals who collected semi-automatic weapons. There amongst the naked girlies was our Adam, and his M14. A memorable quote:
> "It feels good to handle and shoot, and it looks superb – which is also very important to me, be it rifles, cars, women, aircraft or what have you."

Hmm. No mention of Pub Crawls. Yet since his debut Adam's hardly missed an Eric, so I guess we must be somehow impressive.

I have a suspicion that this was the year that Brad hung off the back of the ferry, hoping to 'barefoot waterski' over to the Story Bridge. It didn't work out – he was rather forcibly hauled back aboard – but it may account for his leaving us after that particular hotel, only possibly of his own volition.

It's not unusual to finish a Crawl with a serious case of "the munchies". This time we'd (surprisingly) finished early enough to do something about it. The Adelaide contingent were joined by Rhys, Adam,

Lurch and Jill at an Italian restaurant in the Valley. It *may* have been *Lucky's Trattoria*. I know Tina Thwaites used to work there, and I recall a few serious repasts there, including Robbo's first assault on garlic snails. We may have decided to introduce the South Australians to what was then a semi-legendary venue of Brisbane's *haute cuisine*.

It was this Supplementary Crawl that spawned another enduring legacy. When Gill, Young Dick and I returned to Adelaide we waxed lyrical about what a great time we'd all had. Shortly thereafter it was announced that the old Somerset Hotel on Pulteney Street was to be demolished to make way for, of all things, a new Tax Office.

Both inspired and mortified, we assembled a collection of keen drinkers, mostly from either the ATO or Flinders Uni, and on September 16, 1989 held the first Requiem For The Somerset. I'm quite proud to say that it went on to become an annual event.

Comparing the annual Requiem with the annual Eric reveals something about the two cities, I think. An Eric is usually pretty free-form. We have a date, a planned route, and a couple of traditions like the Yo! call and the t-shirts. In Adelaide the Requiem became a logistical masterpiece. Meal breaks were scheduled. Times were specified for arriving and leaving each bar, and a team of three marshalls each took a shift at blowing a whistle for a two minute warning, then to signal time to move on to the next bar. I got to several, even after I left Adelaide, and was impressed by the level of organization even while people still had a bloody good time.

I don't reckon it'd work up north though.

And eventually it didn't work in South Australia either. The Requiem made it into double figures I think before it finally died. From what I've been told, it became a magnet for trouble, culminating in a year when late in the Crawl someone got thrown through a beautiful old stained glass window in one of the city's more historic bars. Since it was supposed to be about *honouring* pub history, not trashing it, that was the final straw.

Funny thing – when the only rule is "there are no rules", self-discipline just seems to work better. Nothing to rebel against, maybe?

.oOo.

11 1989 – ERIC, THE MOVIE

Ten years! "A Decade Later The Spirits Live On!" proclaimed the t-shirt, proudly displaying an attractive ink drawing of the Belle Vue.

And yet Gill and I wondered if we'd even get there at one stage! The night before we were due to drive north we'd gone for dinner at Gill's parent's place, parking in the car park of the Red Lion next door. Time to go home – I remember standing under a streetlight scratching my head.

"What have you lost?" asks Gill.

"The car. I'm sure it was here when I arrived…"

Faithful Bernadette, loaded with half our clothes and the camping equipment we wanted for the holiday to follow the Crawl, was gone.

Gill's brother Michael made a hero of himself by declaring, "Here's my keys. Take the Escort and we'll find our own way up to the Crawl if we can."

So we trundled north in his little yellow van, learning some of its little eccentricities by trial and error as we went along. From an overnight stop at Gilgandra (I think) we rang home, to find that Bernadette had been located intact, except for a broken window. She'd been abandoned in the charming suburb of Pooraka. Seems someone had wanted to drive home from the pub but couldn't afford a cab.

Michael duly loaded up his car with his girlfriend Marie, best mate Jamie, and a Requiem Crawler named Peter McIntyre (a man who sometimes claimed the credit for introducing Gill to me – I'm not so sure, though I do know we met in the Charles Sturt Tavern where Pete and I often drank). This Peter Mac never bowled leg spin for Australia, either. They headed north with all possible speed, collecting a couple of kangaroos (thank you, Violet Crumple Bar!) and a speeding ticket on their way.

Even when the ticket was being written out, there was surprisingly little reaction from the policeman – around Goondiwindi I think. There was a broken window clearly suggesting a stolen car, interstate plates, a frantic dive to hide the 'funny cigarettes', and a frank admission that no-one in the vehicle actually *owned* it. "It's my brother-in-law's. We're taking it to him in Brisbane."

"Yeah. Right. Here's your ticket. Pay the fine."

Gill and I waited at the Summit Apartments on Leichhardt Street. But before Bernadette's crew arrived we were joined by our other interstate in a little orange station wagon we got to know quite well. Karl's story:

I got a car – Kar Johnston
Two travelling companions from Adelaide
    Richard, doesn't drive
    Liz *(Zaccarra, another theatrical Tax person)* shared the driving
    "it drives well"
Drinking lemon and lime mineral water, "good idea, much better than cola"
I drove into Brisbane
    Trying to find address of motel, trying to find right street
    "There it is, turn left"
    (but we're not in the left lane)
    indicate and swerve, nearly hit another car, swerve back
    Richard: "He's... Really... pissed off"
    Hint: never tell the driver that anyone's really pissed off
    Miss the turn, circle, backtrack, eventually get there, much relief
    Saddle sore.

Sounds like everyone had a fun trip! Michael and the gang arrived soon after, and with great ceremony we exchanged keys. And stories, over beer and steak in the excellent newly opened Beer Garden at the back of the Spring Hill Hotel.

Ten o'clock on October 7 and we were at the Shamrock Hotel in the Valley – all 53 of us! That number continued to swell over several pubs – by the time we hit the Alliance there were well over sixty Crawlers.

Buddy Doyle was one of many returning faces, and he'd come armed with a video camera. *Eric The Movie* is disjointed, odd, frequently coarse, and perhaps cinematography's finest contribution to the old line, "You had to be there to understand."

Judy Fogarty did well to last for the first six or seven pubs, given that she was on crutches from a recent nasty skiing accident.

The 10th Anniversary Crawl was the debut of Gregor Shevtzoff, ex-Adelaidean and old hockey-playing drinking pal of Young Dick. He headed a cheery fellowship of drunks called the Iguanadons, with whom I'd shared many beers on the hill at Adelaide Oval. Gregor has gone on to become a fixture at Erics ever since.

We arrived at the Port Office to find legendary blues guitarist Phil Manning in concert. Phil greeted us with great good humour, and much dancing and fun was had.

There was quite a touching ceremony at the old Belle Vue site. I appreciated the fact that everyone took it seriously – amongst all the laughs and drinks we do still retain a sense of history.

Gill took out the year's Frozen Broccoli Award for her poor suffering feet – first she trod on some broken glass on Leichhardt Street that Peter Mac had to extract at the Sportsman. (Where was I? Good question. Not too sure, actually...) Then she had to retire near the end of the Crawl with *really* nasty blisters.

The Golden Bladder Award went to Party Party Marty somewhere around mid-afternoon, which perhaps indicates that Buddy and I weren't as young as we used to be. He received the trophy proudly, and soon after vanished. Neither Marty nor the trophy have been seen on an Eric since.

We finished up at the Transit Centre (I think – there or the Transcontinental). I know Lurch and I were the last two left at the very end, reliving old glories after whoever else had sensibly gone home. Eventually I staggered back to the Summit and helped finish off Karl and Peter's pizza.

I suspect it was fairly late on Sunday when five Adelaideans squeezed back into the Escort and headed home. I can't think how Canberran Karl happened to be travelling with Liz and Young Dick on the way north, but I know Liz stayed in town, and I'm pretty sure that Richard returned home with Michael and co.

Eric, Gill and I, reunited with Bernadette, happily went off camping at Binna Burra – a nice way to recover from a major event!

.o0o.

12 1990 – A YEAR OF LEGENDS

  Batman returned to the Big Screen. So did Dick Tracy. The Teenage Mutant Ninja Turtles were the In thing. So in an effort to be topical, all of them were worked into this year's t-shirt design.

  Young Dick travelled up from Adelaide with Gill, Eric and I. Karl made a solo trip from Canberra, though I think we met up in a caravan park in Gilgandra and let Bernadette and Kar Johnston keep each other company.

 Just me and Kar Johnston
 A great feeling of release. "At last! Blissful solitude!"
 A trek across Australia – me and my car.
 Not sure if Kar would make it, but no problems
 Afternoon, some rope on the road? A shredded tyre?
    It moves
    It is a snake, across the whole lane
    Unable to react in time, I run over it
    Visions of an angry snake wrapped around something under,
        ready to attack at the next stop
    I survived, though I guess the snake didn't
 Evening, sunset, north NSW, middle of nowhere
    Low rolling country, not flat and not hilly
    Fence along road, fat fence posts
    Seen in passing at 110 kph
    Sitting on a post, a cat in Egyptian statue pose, facing west
    Exactly as though it was relaxing, watching the sunset

  It was a pretty challenging route from the Valley:

Brunswick	Dooley's	Empire
Royal George	Shamrock	Bonaparte's
St Paul's	Alliance	Sportsman

Spring Hill	Rosie's	Embassy
Exchange	Victory	Port Office
Story Bridge	Fridays	Orient
Brisbane	Whistlestop	Crest
Transit	Transcontinental	Majestic
Plaza	Criterion	Wintergarden
Her Majesty's	Berties	Treasury

I'd bought a stock of bright yellow caps somewhere, which were now emblazoned with the words, "I'm A Close Personal Friend Of ERIC". I confess this was an almost direct steal of the name of 'Weird' Al Yankovic's fan club, but it's gone on to be reused at least informally on a pretty regular basis.

The caps were distributed fairly widely, but I don't know whatever happened to them. Mine has long vanished, as I suspect have most. If you've got one, treasure it. They're like hen's teeth now I think.

Neale turned up in a pair of boardshorts printed with a black-and-white psychedelic check pattern that even I found eye-splitting, especially after a few drinks!

At a toyshop (I think) in the Valley, Gregor bought a new mascot for the Crawl – an inflatable stegosaurus christened Steggy. Steggy turned out to be made of pretty durable PVC, surviving pretty much the whole Crawl including fountain swims and what appears in a photo to be a wrestling match with Joe McLaughlin. (I wonder who won?)

Fridays was a posh new bar in the posh new riverside plaza at the bottom of Eagle Street. Over the years it became famous on Pub Crawls for the size and quality of the margheritas served there, but I can't recall if they were available as early as 1990.

Robbo turned up in a bright orange safety helmet, which was later inscribed as the *Official Headbutt Defence Mechanism*. It wasn't as silly an idea as it seems. Years earlier Budgie and I had regular headbutting contests, even getting to the point of charging each other like rhinos. It was all in fun, but Robbo had once made the mistake of unwittingly walking between us at the wrong instant. The results were not pleasant to say the least, especially for Robbo's ribs.

Budgie was no longer an active Crawler, but Young Dick and I had revived the sport to some extent. To this day my nose remains slightly out of shape thanks to an inaccurate Richard headbutt during an early Requiem Crawl. Naturally, Young Dick and I took Robbo's helmet as a challenge. Or we did, until Gill managed to somehow bring us to reason.

As mentioned earlier, the Golden Bladder trophy had disappeared, but the award was still competed for. If memory serves, Young Dick and I eventually settled for an honourable draw. I suspect Gill's rational influence again came into play.

I think we had problems getting into a few of the last pubs on the list. After dark several of the bars around the Mall turned, pumpkin-like, into nightclubs (or so they thought) and had characteristically unimaginative bouncers tasked with keeping riff-raff like us out.

I'm pretty sure we did end up at the Treasury Tavern, though. I think there was a thrash band playing upstairs, and a barely-legal-drinking-age pseudo punk who tried to Shock us by ripping all his clothes off while we enjoyed a last quiet round of drinks. I think he was miffed when the only response he got was a bit of laughter.

Robbo had a pocket notebook on him, and on a page headed *Survivors* the following autographs appear: Robbo, Lurch, Niall, Matt, Dick, Karl, Renoir, Fiona, Kelly – and two incredible scribbles I've never been able to decipher. I have a funny feeling one of them belongs to Eric.

Karl can describe what he remembers of the next day or two (because it's a lot more than I could do!).

Next afternoon, recovery picnic with Renoir's ex-wife and her other half.
    Hoo boy these pub crawls are really something huh
       He: "One year she lost some guy's jacket, and she was real upset"
       Me: lips remain buttoned (d'oh – until now)

Leaving Brisbane, paralleling Renoir and Gillian and Bernadette
    They stopped for petrol, I didn't until later
    For rest of trip, looked out for them, but didn't see them again.
Back in Canberra:
    Renoir: "did you race home or something?"
    Karl: "no, just steady going"
    Gillian: "that can happen, keeping pace with each other"

.oOo.

13 1991 – A HERITAGE LOST

A couple of significant things happened for me early in the year. Eric, Gill and I moved from Adelaide back to Canberra (we were bribed), and Gill and I got married (no bribery required). Quite a few Crawlers came from various parts of Australia to attend the ceremony in the Adelaide Hills.

Marc, Adam, Pete Townley and Lyola Rogers came down from Brisbane; Michael Pegg and Karen Reid from Melbourne; Karl, Rosco and James Townley from Canberra; and of course an Adelaide crew of Young Dick, Peter Mac, Michael and Marie, and a relocated Joe Ziliotto. It puts further emphasis on the bonds that each year's Eric Testimonial helps to reinforce.

I was sitting at my desk on a cold Canberra morning when Rosco brought me that day's *Australian*. There on the front page was a large photo of two of the midnight wreckers, wearing cheesy grins and hard hats.

Above the photo the caption read, Wrecking brothers show students what's left of Brisbane. Underneath that: George and brother Funny at the site of the Belle Vue hotel – a Deen Bros victim in 1979.

There was a headline:
 **Deens strike again,
 this time for heritage**
And a story to the effect that the wrecking business wasn't quite what it used to be, so the Brothers were leading architecture students on a tour of Brisbane historic sites – presumably the ones they'd vandalized...

I'll leave it to you to imagine just how bloody angry I felt. I think a very long lunch was required. But it did at least give me that year's t-shirt design. A slight amendment of the headline to read: "ERIC strikes again…" and inserted into the photo, a symbolically huge Eric plummeting down onto the heads of the grinning 'tour guides'.

There was quite a respectably-sized Canberra contingent that year, who all stayed in the new Summit 2 Apartments across the road from our 1989 home. Eric, Gill and I were joined by Rosco and his housemate Mal (aka Hairy), and travelling separately in Kar Johnson, Karl Johnston and his new girlfriend Fanti. Fanti was an extremely quiet Asian girl, who seldom left her and Karl's room and was never going to be a part of the Pub Crawl. But she made him happy.

 Nice girlfriend
The best, most personal bits will not be reported here – the flesh of a different story

 Left Canberra after work, stayed overnight in Bathurst
 Next day, got to Coonabarabran by lunch, spent afternoon in dinosaur park
 Evening, drove through a couple of towns trying to get as far as possible
"Stop or keep going?" "Keep going."
 Seeing more and more No Vacancy signs
 Did we leave it too late tonight?
 Moree (?), last motel on the right, 'Vacancy'
 An oncoming car
 Impatient, I nipped in front of him into the motel
"That's the last room – now I can turn off the sign"
 That car had pulled in behind us, and we got the last room ahead of them
"Oh well, too bad. You beat us"
 He will probably be less jovial later, when he passes all the No Vacancy signs we saw.

At the time of writing this, the 91 Crawl remains largely mysterious to me. I can't find any notes, or even an invitation. There are very few photographs.

One I think was outside the Brisbane (assuming it ever hosted the

Club Afro-Carib?!?) showing Rhys carrying Eric on a red velvet cushion, flanked by Brian DeSanko, with Gregor, Judy and Hairy visible behind him.

 A couple more from Fridays, where Rosco is wearing The Nose, make it clear that Lurch, Karl and I all decided to wear loud shirts. In my case, over the official t-shirt. For Lurch, the Crawl has become a Loud Shirt Event, with a new one often acquired for the occasion.

 The last photo is one Gregor paid for, taken by a professional photographer in the Criterion Tavern. It shows me, Rosco, Hairy, Neale, Karl, Niall, Ian McLeod, Rhys, Marc, Lurch, Gregor, Paul Kalluschke (on debut?), an ex-Adelaide girl named Lisa Banyard, and a couple of girls no-one seems to recognise. I've an idea it may have been taken during the later part of the day. I think Gill left fairly early to check out some shops, or a market.

 Karl left us as we neared the Crest – a comparatively short climb uphill to the apartment. Still daylight, I remember hiking past a construction site.
A quiet chunder of clear spew, almost crystalline – 100% gin and tonic.
Refreshed I look up and see our motel on the hill to the right.
A fine time to finish, while I'm still humanoid.

I didn't make it to the end
But then again, I had someone to return to this time.

 Alastair tells me the Crawl started at the Grand Chancellor, then to the International and back up along the Spring Hill ridge. He recalls having a pint of Guinness at St. Paul's with Joe McLaughlin before Joe left us.

 Rosco still thinks back on the event a little wistfully. Apparently there was a young lady he was taking some interest in (not too tall, blonde, pretty, and mutually interested it seemed), but somewhere before we hit the Valley Hairy decided he simply couldn't stagger any further. With no idea of where our temporary abode was, or how to get there, he convinced Rosco to get him home. After that, finding and reconnecting with the Crawl seemed utterly impractical, no matter what the attractions!   That's true mateship for you.

Lurch, Al and I are fairly confident that we finished relatively early in the night at Dooley's. It was one of the few places around with Guinness on tap then, and Lurch describes Alastair as "like a kid in a lolly shop".

I reckon that over pints of black gold we were talking about wrestling. Lurch reckons that we were talking in vowels so how would we know?

.o0o.

14 1992 – SCARY!

We were in the grip of the Recession we had to have, I think. Money was tight, even in Canberra!

I was starting to seriously wonder how I'd get to Brisbane with Eric, and was looking seriously at hitch-hiking.

Then a stroke of luck. Into our home came a man who I'll just call The Legend, on loan to Canberra from the Tax Office in Brisbane.. He was great company, liked a drink or three, and needed a room to rent at just the same time as Gill and I needed some supplementary income.

Even better: as part of the conditions of his lengthy 'temporary' transfer he was given a reunion flight home every few months. Late in September he grinned at me over a beer and said, "I don't really want to go back this time. Why don't you be me?"

So I duly presented myself at Canberra airport as Mr. Legend (they didn't bother checking photo ID back then) and with Eric securely in my luggage – I wasn't going to risk him being confiscated from my cabin baggage – away I went.

I was even spared the expense of a motel, thanks to the generous hospitality of Marc and Jenny Hunter. For someone who didn't actually attend an Eric until into the new millennium, Jenny has been a notable part of Crawl history.

The tight finances were also reflected in the Crawl invitation.

No t-shirts this year due to the H.E.T. Syndrome (Harsh Economic Times). Dress to be loud and/or comfortable.

As a small compensation though, I prepared the first Pub Crawl badges, using a stack of conference name tags with an insert based on the invitation: on dark red stock – **Eric the Thirteenth – The Night No-one Comes Home SOBER!**

(Yes, I think the movie *Friday The 13th* was probably fresh in my memory.)

Loud and/or comfortable was taken as a challenge by many. Lurch made another statement to his claim to the title of Master of the Loud Shirt. Every year Jill seems to manage an effort of either shopping or sewing excellence, although her husband does sometimes claim to do his own shopping. Hmm...

I'd picked up a fluorescent multi-coloured tie dyed shirt that I dearly loved, and that made a few subsequent appearances. Matt Taylor wore an exquisite pair of pink and purple paisley pants (say *that* six times quickly!) and Paul (PK) Kalluschke was dapper in a black and white full gangster suit.

Gary Thwaites made a fleeting appearance with new son Calum. Sadly we haven't seen much of Gary since, though I believe Calum is now a practicing lawyer. (I wonder what happens if they don't practice?) Also doing the parent thing was Jill Smith-Moore carrying a young Sophie who made it to the second pub before waving bye-bye to Daddy. By day's end she was possibly walking better than he was.

By this time I was finally starting to get over my anti-Expo gripe, and we actually set off from the Ship Inn on October 3. The day's list read:

Ship Inn	Plough	Terminus
Criterion	Majestic	Transcontinental
Transit	Crest	Whistlestop
Spring Hill	Actress & Bishop	St Pauls
Brisbane	Orient	Fridays
Story Bridge	Port Office	Heritage
Exchange	Victory	Embassy
Rosies	Her Majesty's	Wintergarden

Treasury   Berties
27: wherever you can afford a drink

It seemed we'd learned little from the previous year's experience, with so many Mall area bars listed late in the proceedings.

The City Plaza, sometimes loved and sometimes maligned, had finally ceased to be. It was simply taken over by shops and offices. I can't say it was missed for its architectural beauty, but it was always a shame to note any regular port of call falling off the Available list.

We never minded that the Alliance frequently operated as Brisbane's leading gay bar. Sexual preference has never mattered to us – just the love of a good time. This pub was often very good to us, even under a succession of owners. That didn't change, even when it took on the new title of The Actress & The Bishop (in joke terms, a popular d-Alliance?). The name only name only lasted for a few years, but it remains one of my favourite monikers for a pub anywhere in the world.

Another year, another ferry trip or two. Our departure was delayed because so many of us had crowded onto the top deck of the ferry. Marc remembers the worried ferry driver asking people to "please come downstairs as there's not enough ballast". Apparently he feared a capsize. The biggest problem was that we couldn't actually *hear* him over the loudspeaker. Not until after we'd finished *Gilligan's Island*, at least!

We were a little intimidated at first by the Heritage at the bottom of Edward Street. It was just so *elegant*! Surely they wouldn't let an unruly mob like us in without a struggle? I mean, we had a running battle with the Victory for many years, and it's a LONG way down the social ladder from a class act like the Heritage.

But I'm pleased to report that we've never been made anything less than very welcome. Even when there have been weddings and other functions happening, they've dealt with us courteously and efficiently, slotting us in around people and things so we had a good time without disrupting anyone else's enjoyment of their day. Well, there was this *one* wedding in '99 – I'll get to that later.

Harsh economic times notwithstanding, we proved up to the task of making our own entertainment. According to my diary the 1992

Testimonial was "quite possibly the friendliest, most jovial in the annals of Ericdom." Even if we *didn't* have much paraphernalia.

And I made it home to Canberra safely, returning Mr. Legend's identity to him intact. He never did get to an Eric, much to my regret, and died quite suddenly some years later. A good mate, still much missed. There are too many of them over forty years.

.o0o.

15 1993 – IMAGES

Another year, another new address… Now Eric, Gill and I were Victorians. We'd moved to Beechworth, an old gold mining town at the foot of snow country.

It was a town steeped in Australian history, being one of the pivotal locales in the Kelly Gang story, and living there quickly accelerated my appreciation of things past.

I dusted off my old sketch pads and found a drawing I'd done years earlier – a rough depiction of the demolished ruin of the Belle Vue, in the far foreground of which stood a beer glass. Through that, in a finer hand I'd drawn the façade of the pub as it had been before the Deens moved in in April '79.

It seemed an effective symbol, and gave us the year's t-shirt design. *14 Years On: Through A Glass DARKLY.* A couple of special editions were created for Gregor's old drinking squad, with the addition of a little dinosaur and the words "Iguanodon On Crawl".

The pleasantly cool conditions of the Supplementary Crawl in '89 had stuck in the memory. In an effort to revisit that weather July 10 was chosen as this year's date.

Once again we set ourselves a challenge.
```
    Gabba               Recovery            Morrison
    Clarence Corner     Kelly's             Ship Inn
    Plough              Boardwalk (ferry)   Fridays
    Orient              Brisbane            St Paul's
    Actress & Bishop    Sportsman           Spring Hill
    Whistlestop         Fihelly's Arms      Crest
    Transit             Transcontinental    Majestic
```

Legends	Criterion	Treasury
Lands Office	Metropolis *(Myers)*	Lennons
Britannia	Wintergarden	Her Majesty's
Rosies	Embassy	Exchange
Victory	Port Office	Heritage

And finally over the water to the Story Bridge.

Just to add to the challenge, the Bridge had been chosen as last because the date happened to coincide with their annual Festival of Australian Beers.

The Queensland Tourism Bureau was having one of its intermittent bouts of aggressive marketing, and were then using the remarkably meaningless catchphrase "Yo! Queensland!" Beyond sniggering a bit at it, I hadn't given the campaign much thought. Until we got to the Ship Inn, that is. On the footpath outside the front door we found a large promotional prop, left looking somewhat forlorn all by itself. (Possibly the workmen charged with its care were having A Quiet One.)

The prop was a giant word balloon, about a metre and a half tall. Emblazoned on a black background, in large friendly yellow letters was the word YO! Suddenly it dawned on us – it was the Pub Crawl Call To Arms. *WE* were the image that Queensland Tourism was trying to promote!

An appropriate photo of yours truly in full cry with visible sound effect was duly taken, and we went on our way with new respect for the insight of the Government's highly paid consultants. Even so, I don't think that particular campaign lasted long.

I'm sure it's only a matter of accidental circumstance, but the photos I have of the '93 Crawl show Sue McKew in the arms of a succession of different blokes. Sue's always been regarded as a paragon of virtue so I'm *quite* sure she wasn't actually flirting with every male on the event.

I can pretty much vouch for that fact, as one of the photos shows Sue with me, and I reckon I would remember if she had ever flirted seriously with me. It just goes to show how the camera can mislead. I'm glad I haven't only had photographs on which to base this book, or who knows what leaps of interpretation I might have made?

Finishing up at a crowded Beer Festival meant a rather more chaotic ending than usual. Most years, a few survivors are left getting a bit mellow and reflective, mostly with only ourselves for company. Not this time, what with queuing for tickets for each drink, and being spoilt for choice from a whole spectrum of good (and not-so-good) stuff on offer.

Late in the evening, a taxi left the Story Bridge bearing PK, Matt Walker, Rocky and his girlfriend. Matt expressed an interest in 'kicking on' so he was dropped off at a party the others knew about. It seemed like quite a fun affair. There were a lot of really good-looking blokes there, many of whom seemed to be very *close*. Slowly it dawned on Matt's Crawl-befogged brain that there were no women at the party...

I believe he got home soon after, suddenly a bit more sober.

.o0o.

16 1994 – MORE SINGIN' IN THE RAIN

'93 had gone so well it was decided not to mess with things too much. The July date was kept – Saturday the 9th this time. The itinerary was very similar too, extended only slightly by the addition of the Aussie Nash (Australian National, for the purist) and the Broadway before we made it to the Gabba Hotel, and the insertion of Chancellors On The Park (posh new place where the City View used to be) and the International in between the Spring Hill and the Whistlestop.

In honour of the fifteenth anniversary event I added a little silver trim to the t-shirt – an otherwise simple depiction of Eric against a background of mottos and phrases from previous Crawl history.

The Aussie Nash proved a popular choice as a starting point when it was found to have Guinness on tap. A noble breakfast for many, with more protein than a steak-and-egg sandwich in every pint.

Amongst the enthusiastic starters were David and Val Weatherley, with their daughter Danielle. David and Val were quite insistent that they weren't along as chaperones – they liked the sound of the Crawl and had come for a good time. They were as good as their word, too. Danielle moved to England not too long after (and is still our Official UK Crawl Liaison), but her parents attended plenty more Erics without her!

Also present, for the only time so far, were *two* Robinson brothers – Robbo and his younger brother Jack. Robbo looked particularly splendid in a black and gold smoking jacket. I simply can't agree with the nameless Philistine who suggested that it looked like it had been made from the wallpaper of a Chinese restaurant!

The first two pubs' visitors also included the latest addition to Lurch's clan – like the younger Robinson also named Jack. Even at that tender age he had just about as much hair as his father – an equation that has only shifted in his favour with time. There are some things that the camera does *not* mislead about.

There was Adult Entertainment happening on the TV at the Recovery Hotel, which appeared to consist mostly of a half-naked young lady squirming on the face of a fat drunk. This prompted the comment, "Some men will eat anything."

The Morrison disappointed us by being closed during daylight hours. The name of their new restaurant seemed apt – *Fiasco's*.

Undaunted, we marched into the next pub, which seemed by its signage to be having trouble deciding whether to call itself Kelly's or O'Grady's. Either way, they brewed their own beer and did a pretty good job of it, too.

I don't know if he was kidding himself or not, but there was an old chap in the bar there who looked at us as we arrived and exclaimed, "I remember you lot!" Then again, we meet a lot of barflys every year – they only meet one company of Eric's friends.

After years of clement weather, we finally had a Crawl with a fair bit of wet stuff on our outsides as well as insides. The rain didn't really start until we were in the Southbank precinct, by which time we were sufficiently on our way to not care.

My major irritation was at the later discovery that my extravagant tie-dye from 1992 had run alarmingly into the 15th Anniversary t-shirt I was wearing underneath. Mutter, grumble.

During our stay at Friday's there was finally some sort of formal recognition of Cathy Moss's birthday, which she'd been enthusiastically reminding everyone of. Some kind person arranged a party pie for her, into which had been stuck a satay skewer that was then lit to do service as a candle. She looks pretty impressed in the photo.

The Frozen Broccoli Award had quietly slipped into disuse over the past couple of years, but its memory was revived in the Sportsman when Iguanodon Brian made an inebriated hash of trying to open his own umbrella. He had a bloody good go (and I choose my words carefully there) at slicing his hand in two. Luckily Danielle had not long gotten her first aid certificate, and proudly showed off her new skills in bandaging his paw back together. I don't think Brian was feeling any pain by that stage anyway.

We were starting to straggle a bit by the time we got to Chancellors atop Spring Hill. One of the last people there, I realised that many of our number were already down the hill at the Central Station bars, and if we didn't hurry up there could be an irretrievable logistics breakdown. There were a handful of us preparing to try a sprint downhill, when Larry said, "Wait! Leave it to me!"

He dashed across the street to where a Council works gang were on a smoko break. We followed, and got there in time to hear the boss being asked by one of his men, "This bloke wants a ride on the loader. He's on a Pub Crawl. What do I tell him?"
"Is he gonna pay ya?"
"Yeah."
"Take 'em, ya fool!"

So, with me clutching Eric very carefully, we clambered onto whatever positions we could find on the front end loader, and were taken along Wickham Terrace and Upper Edward Street to the railway station. Some of our crew were already on the footpath about to enter Fihelly's Arms, and were suitably gobsmacked. The five of us dashed upstairs and had a very quick drink with the others in the Whistlestop, and were able to get the Crawl back 'on track' from there.

Sometimes Larry really didn't deserve the "Larry the Loser" nickname he was often tagged with. Oh sure, a taxi would have been quicker, and I daresay cheaper, but it wouldn't have added so much to the Eric legend, would it?

David's recollection of the Port Office is of our meeting up with a buck's party in the front bar. A streaker ran through the crowd alarming, or rather, amusing the girls. Out in the courtyard was a singer/guitarist who graciously allowed his act to be 'taken over' by yours truly. I'm not sure how much choice he was given... To considerable acclamation from the assembled Crawl I somehow fitted the words of *Gilligan's Island* to the tune of *Stairway To Heaven*.

 I'm pretty sure that the final ferry trip across to the Story Bridge was, er... a bridge too far for many. There's a rather sweet photo of Vanessa's sister Cuscus asleep in the oversized wooden chair outside the Port Office beer garden, Eric on his cushion in her lap.

 Somewhere along the way, the rain stopped. I think. It seems likely we neither noticed nor cared much by then.

.o0o.

17 1995 – SMART CASUAL ATTIRE

Gill and I brought Eric up to Queensland a few days early, feeling that we needed a short holiday to build up our strength before the event, due on July 15.

Revelling in the Sunshine State's winter, we headed for Hervey Bay. To our delight, at Shelley Beach we found Eric Street. Mainstream recognition at last!

With our batteries recharged we returned to Brisbane, and our room at Marc and Jenny's.

For reasons I don't recollect there were no official t-shirts in 1995. Several of us rose to new heights of sartorial elegance to compensate. Ian McLeod has a well known and well worn bright blue suit coat that has graced numerous Crawls.

Perhaps that coat was some sort of subliminal inspiration for Adam and I, suited at opposite ends of the elegance spectrum. He was dapper in a black dinner suit. I like to think my suit had more character. It's a wide boy number in blue and white striped seersucker. In recognition of the historical context of an Eric Crawl I wore it over my old View World Hotel *Last Drinks* t-shirt from before Expo.

Also looking pretty nifty was our host Marc, his 86 t-shirt teamed with a groovy velour and paisley ensemble.

Marc and PK did their bit to overcome the lack of uniformity in attire by producing their first in a continuing series of Crawl badges, this one in traditional Fourex colours.

Returning from Canberra was an old friend, not alone this time either.

Karl was now married. After a year's absence it was like he'd never been away. And it was still an adventure.

Rebecca and Karl
Kar Johnston died en route
> Towed to a garage in Corowa
>> Battery lead, easily fixed, and on the road again. Whew

Motel in Brisbane close to both starting and ending (Story Bridge) pub

...Eric...

We made it to the end, somehow
Après Eric, staggering back to motel
> Hungry (a motif?)
> 24 hour corner shop
> After much squinting at wares, bought sliced salami and one onion
> Rebecca: "That man (shopkeeper) was looking at you"
> Late night fryup
> Evil residue next morning, in wok and in me.

It was a creative route, beginning and ending, as Karl said, at the Story Bridge. I think we may have travelled from one ferry terminal through town, up Spring Hill and back down again to the other ferry. Certainly I have neither memory nor photographic evidence of being in either the Valley or South Brisbane.

A blast from the past was the return to our ranks of Lyola, last seen On Crawl in 1983. This time she'd brought her husband Pete, a long-standing friend to several of us, but who'd somehow never made it onto an Eric before.

At some point of mid-afternoon we approached the Crest, now calling itself Picasso's, and seeming more upmarket than ever. The sign on the door said: *Dress Smart Casual*. Most of the crew figured we wouldn't have the proverbial snowball's chance in Hell of getting in, and weren't going to bother trying. Undeterred by the sign, Gregor and I strode straight in.

My outfit you already know about. Gregor certainly fitted the 'Casual' requirement, in an old Requiem shirt, furry Russian hat and rather worn pullover. I admit we were mildly surprised when there were absolutely no objections to our appearance – in fact the barman took a photo of the two of us in front of the Dress Code sign. Naturally, we called the rest of the Crawl in, and Picasso's bar take for the afternoon was dramatically improved.

Gregor looks rather less smart in the final photo of the day. He's slumped on the footpath outside the Story Bridge's Bombshelter Bar, alongside Ian McLeod and Niall, both of whom look similarly like... well, like they're at the end of a Pub Crawl.

My only postscript pertains to Gill's and my drive back south. The chilly weather meant that we had the heater on in the car as we travelled. Eric sat on the shelf behind the back seat, still on his cushion. The same cushion that had, as usual, copped the spillage of the many and varied libations poured on the Guest of Honour during his Crawl.

As we drove we eventually noticed that the rear window was steaming up, and there was a definite 'hotel floor' aroma starting to fill the car. The heater was gradually turning the contents of the cushion to steam, and not very pleasant steam at that. Never mind the cold and occasional rain – we drove with the back windows down for as long as we possibly could!

.o0o.

18 1996 – JUDY TAKES CHARGE

96 was a pretty difficult year for me. I was coming to terms with my Dad's death, I had a few worrying medical issues of my own, work came in sporadic but intensive bursts – there were a collection of stresses that you don't need to know about, but which took a lot of my attention away from the annual testimonial for my little masonry pal.

Judy Fogarty (the artist earlier known as Frog) stepped into the breach in fine style, and did a great deal of the organizing. To everyone's delight though, it wasn't *over*-organised. As noted a few chapters ago, I don't believe that the Adelaide level of Pub Crawl management would work with the Friends of Eric.

We were to travel from the Gabba to Southbank, then across the river to the Story Bridge and back to the Port Office (the invitation considerately included ferry times). An amble through the bottom end of town, then down into the Valley to end up at Dooley's.

Perhaps the most valuable innovation that Judy came up with was to publicise a mobile phone number (**modern mobile communications technology**) for the benefit of any strays who needed to catch up with us further up the track.

These nifty inventions would have been bloody handy on plenty of previous occasions as we lost Crawlers, or they lost us, in an alcoholic haze.

On a footpath somewhere Sue McKew found the name ERIC written in chalk. It sparked a long conversation between Alastair and I about the famous 'Eternity' graffiti that Arthur Stace wrote (in beautiful copperplate handwriting) all over Sydney between 1932 and 1967. We never saw any more ERIC inscriptions though. Nor wrote any.

It was still fairly early in the evening when we arrived at the Wickham, but there was already a good crowd of their regular patrons in attendance. Marc and PK slipped off their t-shirts and wore only their leather vests (above the waist, that is) so as to fit in.

Prominent in the bar was a coin-operated ski machine. You climbed onto a pair of skis mounted, like the poles, on a sort of universal joint arrangement in front of a big screen. Insert money, and the video screen displays the slope you're dashing down.

Wayne Hunter is a serious snow enthusiast, and just *had* to have a go. His efforts attracted an appreciative crowd of the Wickham's regulars, clustered in a semi-circle behind him.

Wayne's better half Anne fair glowed with pride. "They really like his form, don't they?" she said to me, beaming.

"You're not kidding," I replied with an evil laugh.

"What do you mean?" asked Anne, all innocence.

In explanation I led her to a position behind Wayne, where we shared in the view of his pert buttocks wiggling in his tight jeans like two cats in a small sack.

"This is a gay bar," I pointed out calmly.

Poor Wayne wasn't quite sure why his beloved peremptorily whisked him off the machine when he'd been "doing so well!" We didn't have the heart to tell him until several pubs later, when we could finally explain without laughing.

I think it was in the Empire that I wandered into the Men's room and was impressed by the fact that all of the lights were ultra-violet fluorescent tubes. "Wow! Black lights in the john – this is a *real* party pub!" I was rather disappointed to learn I was only 'kind-of' right, it was a party pub of sorts, but the UV lights weren't for partying under.

They were to make it hard for intravenous drug users to find their veins when shooting up. Suddenly I felt old.

A curious thing happened when we got to Dooley's at the end of the Crawl. They didn't allow hats to be worn inside, and insisted that we remove our various caps and chapeaux.

It was a curious mix of headgear. Robbo and Rhys wore wide-brimmed black hats (Robbo's with the inspiring motto *Ebrio Ergo Sum* painted on – 'I drink therefore I am', for those who don't speak Latin). Alastair had a respectable white flat cap, and Marc an elaborate half fez that was a bit like a soft but gaudy pill box.

Matt Taylor wore a very cool knitted Rasta hat complete with fake dreadlocks. It had looked good on Lurch earlier, especially when teamed with the brick-carrier's red nose. My sun protection was an old grey Stetson, chosen because of its resemblance to the hat I wore on the very first Crawl. It was of the style last regularly seen in the great 1960s/70s Australian TV crime show *Homicide*. Not to be confused with the much later US show of the same name which had more 'grit' but a lot less charm.

All of us were required to go bare-headed into the bar – all except one. The exception was Paul Kalluschke, who was allowed to enter wearing his two-foot-high multi-coloured clown's top hat. We never did work out if they thought he was to be feared or pitied. Gill suggested that he was being used as an example to other patrons.

.o0o.

19 1997 – THE FIRST ADULT ERIC

Eric turning 18 conjured up all sorts of interesting possibilities for artwork. I managed to resist all of them.

The Victorian experience behind us, Eric, Gill and I were back in South Australia, nestled in the Adelaide Hills in Hahndorf. Unfortunately Eric and I were the only members of the family able to make the trek north this time.

The invitation that I sent opened with the lines:
Let's go crawlin' now
Everybody's learnin' how
Come on this year's ERIC with me...

Clearly I was on a Beach Boys kick. Of course. Hahndorf has such a close relationship with surfing. (It's in the hills – you cannot see or smell a beach for many miles.)

A Brisbane-sourced invitation read:
Yes, having survived the perils of childhood and a spotty adolescence, Eric is at last legal. And to celebrate he wants a day of your time to have a drink at each of thirty pubs and live to tell the young folks... First drinks at 10:00 am, the last when you can cram 'em down. Be there or be square!

In a general sense, the route was a reversal of the '96 version:

Dooley's	Empire	Royal George
Deck Bar	Prince Consort	Wickham
Shamrock	Bonaparte's	Spring Hill
Alliance	Fihelly's Arms	Brisbane
Orient	Fridays	Story Bridge
Port Office	Heritage	City Rowers

Victory	Charlotte's	Embassy
Rosie's	Her Majesty's	Wintergarden
Criterion	Crest	Transit Centre
Transcontinental	Lands Office	Treasury
Sly Fox		

Charlotte's was an extremely short-lived name for the hotel more usually known as the Exchange, Stock Exchange or Stockie. Rather a shame really – the actual stock exchange hasn't been nearby for years, and there's a very old tradition of pubs being named for British Royalty.

Queen Charlotte (for whom the street, then the pub, were named) was the wife of George III. She married the King in 1761, and survived as Queen until 1818. There was a very strong African strain in Charlotte's bloodline, although it was apparently regarded as impolite to mention that it was obvious in some of her features. She did get involved in the anti-slavery movement that was starting to gain acceptance, and helped establish Kew Gardens – still well worth a visit for plant lovers visiting England.

The old Majestic, maligned as a Carlton pub in early Crawl days, but a familiar part of the George Street landscape for many years, was the latest casualty of "progress" in Brisbane. Towards the end of its life the Lounge Bar was converted into the delightfully tacky Big Kahuna Bar. Unfortunately it was gone too soon to make it onto a Crawl.

I do remember my Dad having to be "locked up" in the Majestic while a juror on the Whiskey-A-GoGo firebombing murder trial in the '70s. A non-drinker since his army days, he collected the paper umbrellas from female jurors' cocktails as souvenirs for me. I think I've still got one stashed away.

The City Rowers was more in the nature of a trendy dance club than a bar by the time we got there, just around sundown I think. There were an awful lot of people there who looked like they spent most of the week in school uniforms (one way or another). Hardly surprisingly, none of them were convinced to tag along with us for the rest of the way, although I think that surprised and disappointed Dave.

The Sly Fox was a short-lived trendy name for the old Terminus at the Southbank end of Victoria Bridge. Finishing there was a courageous call, motivated by their advertising "Brisbane's only Vodka Bar!"

Of course, that's where we aimed for. To our puzzlement, the Vodka Bar actually seemed to stock more varieties of schnapps than vodka. Nonetheless, several of us determinedly made our way through most, if not all of their list.

After a full day's Pub Crawling, that stands as a remarkable feat of stubbornness, determination, and sheer bloody stupidity. Among the hazy memories are Lurch playing pool with Adam and Rhys, and Paul K and Nicci both checking out the comparative acoustics of the Mens' and Ladies' toilets. I'm not going to ask how.

The only negative at the Sly Fox was their refusal to allow entry to Rocky – our Sri Lankan percussionist – who evidently had some 'prior form' in the bar. A couple of other West End locals promptly called a boycott and left. Those of us already inside missed what had happened and drank on in blissful ignorance until much later, by which time it was far too late for us to do anything helpful or otherwise.

Rocky's presence on several mid-to-late 90s Erics carries a slightly odd story in itself. He'd come along as a friend of Gregor's. Anyone who drinks at the Boundary Hotel in West End is likely to be a friend of Gregor's. But he was surprised to be instantly recognised.

Way back in about 1982 Robbo and I had worked as stage crew for a fund-raising concert run by *A*M*U*S*E - Artists and Musicians United for Safe Energy*. On the whole, if I'm honest it was pretty ordinary, but one outstanding performance came from this wiry little dark guy who played <u>the best</u> bongos and congas I'd ever heard.

During and after the show over a few drinks he introduced himself to us as Rocky. The name stuck in my memory because he was about as unlike Sylvester Stallone as a man can look. A decade and a half later, I walked up to him and said, "I'd wondered whatever happened to you..."

As is probably the case most years, the day after the Pub Crawl brought challenges for some. I'm indebted to Alastair Wallace for the following story.

The week after the event, my wife Margaret and I were visiting friends of ours in Ipswich. Lurch's daughter Sophie just happened to be in Year 1 at school, and her teacher just happened to be the person we were visiting.

For 'News' on the Monday following the Crawl, little Sophie told her class that Mummy had had to warn her and her little brother Jack that Daddy had a headache and he was not – under any circumstances and for any reasons – to be disturbed!

They're good kids. I'm *sure* they obeyed.

.o0o.

20 1998 – SHOWTIME!

For any of you not from Brisbane, I'll quickly explain that early August is always the season for the Royal National Association Exhibition – the Show, or more commonly, the Ekka.

This is promoted as Party Time for the city, so I suppose it was inevitable that we'd eventually weaken and schedule an Eric to coincide.

To my delight, Gill was able to make the trip with Eric and I this time, and we were again made welcome by Marc and Jenny.

T-shirts were back on the agenda at last – a simple design of Eric and his red nose. The logo for the year, as befitting the timing, was *Proud To Be Making An Exhibition Of Myself*.

The eighth of the eighth was the designated date, and Val Weatherley got the guernsey for compiling this year's route.

Val opted for a new starting point in the Valley, based largely I suspect on the pub's name: The Rat. In essence, though, it was a similar route to '97.

Jill brought Jack and Sophie along to farewell their Dad again. A particularly commendable effort as she was not at all well that day. She'd put on a brave face, so Lurch didn't discover until that night how sick she really was – I will record here that he felt appropriately guilty, even though he wasn't to know at the time.

Paul K and Marc both had their heads shaved before the Crawl. I *hope* it was for charity, because if it was done to enhance their looks it was an abject failure. I still reckon that God disguises so many heads with hair for a good reason. I know my head is in that category!

There is a photo of Matt Taylor with a bunch of Crawlers wearing Ekka silly hats and masks, which are obviously effective disguises as I haven't worked out who any of those people are.

We added the Jubilee to our list as we went along. This is sometimes fine (occasionally dodgy) old pub down near the Exhibition Grounds, so it was an appropriate inclusion. Several Crawlers played pool in the covered courtyard out the back. I'd never seen so many pool tables covered with bright blue felt.

In what may have been a misguided attempt at exercise we tried walking from the Valley over the Story Bridge to the hotel of the same name. Not a popular move, as it turned out: a long dry spell, and the bridge crossing itself was an unpleasant experience for those of us who suffer from acrophobia (fear of heights).

Fairly late in the event we found ourselves at a Karaoke Bar in the Crest. We were sharing the place with a Hen's Night, I believe, and there were probably attempts by some to lure some drunken women along with us. Don't know that anyone had any success, though.

The Karaoke was another opportunity to murder *Gilligan's Island*. This time it was to the tune of *House Of The Rising Sun*. It's amazing what shapes those lyrics can be forced into! I then dragged Lurch onto the stage with me, I suspect to showcase a voice that made mine sound comparatively good.

Another late finish at the Sly Fox. I think I loaded Lurch into a cab, then decided to have "just one more vodka".

It was past midnight, I think, when I started walking back to Marc and Jenny's place. Struck by hunger pangs I wandered into an all-night convenience store. The sub-continental-looking shopkeeper (who, in my head, I immediately christened "Apu") seemed deeply disturbed by Eric sitting placidly on his black cushion on the counter.

I tried to explain his story, and about the Belle Vue, and the Deens, but I don't think it was helping. If the man's look had been any more blank I could have ruled lines on it and written a short story.

As I left the shop, contentedly munching my microwaved hot dog, I was joined by two blokes I hadn't noticed hanging around outside the front door.

They evidently had immediately picked me to be their best friend, and staggered along Boundary Street with Eric and I. Maybe they were homeless, I don't know, but they gave every indication of intending to accompany me all the way to wherever I was headed, and settle there themselves.

I may have been on the far side of a serious Pub Crawl, but even I knew that this was not likely to be terrifically popular with Gill, far less Jenny and Marc. I proceeded to become convincingly disoriented and took some really interesting byways in the hope that they'd get bored and wander off.

That didn't look like happening, and I'd pretty much run out of ideas when a taxi pulled up alongside us. The passenger door opened, and out fell a kid who looked like he was on his way home from his first high school Senior Social – crumpled remains of a good shirt, tie hanging loose, trousers damp and stained. The boy shoved a fistful of money at the cabbie and said something like, "Yeah. Right here. Thanks."

The eyes of my two companions lit up, and suddenly they had a new best friend. I left the three of them staggering away in the opposite direction from me, the blind leading the blind.

The whole episode added an hour or two to my walk. The next morning I had some serious explaining to do about why I was home so late. I'd like to think I was believed – I really couldn't make that story up!

.oOo.

21 1999 – TREATING ZYMOCENOSILICAPHOBIA

The nasty big Z word above means 'the morbid fear of an empty beer glass'. Could there be any condition for which a Pub Crawl is a better treatment?

After over a decade of moving all over Australia, Eric finally came back to Brisbane when Gill and I moved north. A new adventure for Gill, a wheel turning full circle for the Half-a-Brick and me.

One of the best things about the move was having a ready-made social life to settle into – all of the friends who'd been retained and made throughout the annual 'pilgrimages'.

This time there would be no travel plans to make – we were Locals.

It was a tough call, trying to decide whether to make a fuss over either the twentieth or twenty-first year of Ericing. It seemed too much to attempt to call successive years Major Events.

We'd tried to make the tenth and fifteenth anniversaries a bit special, so there was a case for 1999. But there's something special and traditional about celebrating a 21st, too.

My thought process went something like this – anniversaries are for things, birthdays are for individuals. The Pub Crawl has become an institution and a damned fine one at that, but it wouldn't exist without the individual that is Eric The Half-a-Brick. After all this time, I certainly think of him as having a personality of his own. I'm pretty sure I've seen him smile on plenty of occasions!

So birthday it would be. 1999 would be 'just another' Pub Crawl.

Of course, in saying that I have to admit that there's no such thing. Each is special in its own way, in both its planning and how it eventuates.

Judy had a great idea for the 20th Eric shirt: base the design on the 20th Century Fox logo. That challenge appealed to the graphic artist in me, so I set about with a will to make the *20th Eric Pub Crawl* logo. I reckon it turned out pretty well, too. We chose to make it a polo shirt, thinking that the collar might help us get past some security. A nice thought… The logo also made its way onto the year's badges.

A few other elements found their way into the finished product of the shirt, like the phobia reference above. On the sleeve was the inscription **Trample the weak… Hurdle the dead!**

I can't recall now where I found that particular quote, but I know when I saw it I immediately thought of Eric. It appealed to many of us. Judy liked it enough to put it on the signature block of her emails. She was working then for the recently elected Federal Member based in Rockhampton. Somehow a piece of e-correspondence from the electorate office found its way to the *Age* newspaper in Melbourne. A columnist there, knowing nothing of Eric, ran a short paragraph expressing just a little concern about the apparent attitude of the staff in the office of the Federal Member For Capricornia.

Lurch had bravely volunteered to plan the route for this year, and I bravely volunteered to help with the reconnaissance. After a couple of years of Valley starts, we decided to return to the south side.

Both of us had long had a soft spot for the Red Brick Hotel on Annerley Road. Just the name had something appealing about it. Unfortunately by 1999 the name had changed to Burke's Hotel. Fortunately most of the ambience hadn't changed (if you ignored the poker machine lounge, and we tried to). We were much encouraged on our 'scouting mission' there, and it proved a popular spot from which to launch on October 16.

We devised a route that, for variety's sake missed some familiar inner-city bars in favour of a loop through Spring Hill. From Burke's we travelled:

Clarence Corner	Kelly's	Ship Inn
Boulevard	Plough	ferry to Fridays
ferry to Story Bridge	ferry to Heritage	Victory
Stock Exchange	Rosies	Fihelly's Arms
Whistlestop	Brisbane	Orient
Bonaparte's	Alliance	Sportsman
Spring Hill	Chancellors	Normanby
LA	Caxton	Transcontinental
Transit Centre		

You'll note there were THREE ferry trips scheduled. No surprise that the regular choral sessions as we crossed the river were usually led by Lurch and me, and Gregor.

There's been a growing tradition of 'family ties' on Crawls. The Hunter brothers; the Robinsons; Gill's brother Mick returning for the 20th accompanied by his new girlfriend who in turn met up with *her* brother; David, Val and Danielle; Nicci and Sandra... This year it was Cathy Moss' turn as her Mum came along for the ride. We discovered that having a good time is clearly an inherited trait, as both Moss ladies were fun to be around as they very obviously enjoyed themselves.

On the subject of mothers, the first person to bring their offspring on a Crawl – Catherine Collins of the 'class of 83' – rejoined us. This time she *didn't* bring Aaron, or the little wagon. (I do wonder if Aaron would have been any better behaved.)

Over the year's the little wagon's place has been taken by a succession of plush cushions. Every few years these are retired when the accumulated effects of the annual flood of drinks given to Eric become too much to wash out. For a while Lurch kept one red velvet cushion at home, still complete with the ribbons that acted as Eric's 'seatbelts'. Sophie used it as a nest for a bird marionette. I wonder if it was a gannet? (Famously from a Monty Python sketch, they wet their nests.)

While we were in Fridays Alastair and I were having a conversation

about Gill with Catherine. As Al puts it:
> We were extolling Gill's virtues mightily, to which the woman said to Renoir, "I'd really like to meet your wife."
> The conversation over, Catherine turned to the woman sitting quietly beside her and introduced herself. "And who are you?" she asked.
> "Renoir's wife."

Toni von Finglebumm-Smythe was living somewhere around Canberra by 1999. We don't see her much so it was an unexpected bonus to find that she and her new parner Helen were visiting Brisbane at just the right time to join us. Prior engagements meant that it wasn't a long stay, but it's always good to renew old friendships.

Shortly after we left Burke's we passed a little clutch of small shops. A couple of shopkeepers stood in close discussion on the footpath, watching us go by. One was heard to remark to the other, "It must be some kind of convention." I'm reminded of Dr. Frank-n-Furter's line in *The Rocky Horror Picture Show* about an unconventional convention.

In Kelly's Wayne took pains to point out to anyone listening that Anne had left a full inch of beer in only the third pub. After the ski machine incident a few years earlier you'd think he might have learned some discretion, eh?

Passing through the Southbank markets on the way to the Plough, a couple of the lads decided to invest in 'temporary tattoos'. Paul K and Wayne had Chinese characters embellished on their necks.

They were told they represented 'peace' and 'happiness' or something like that. I don't speak the language so I don't know, but I did notice a few Asian people snickering at them later. Maybe Pub Crawls are intrinsically amusing (they certainly are for the people *on* them), or maybe the boys actually wore the Mandarin for "I'm with Stupid" and "I'm Stupid".

Paul K also had a bar code emblazoned on the back of his head. He was quite disappointed when he presented himself at a convenience store much later in the night and found that he couldn't actually be scanned. So much for the new high-tech version of Brad's old Brain Scanner!

Leaving the Plough Inn Cathy almost literally collided with her straight-laced Aunty Ivy, who exclaimed, "Oh! What are you doing here?"

The reply from the self confessed Divine Fabulous & Wonderful One: "Oh... ahh... um... I'm on a... er... Pub Crawl. Mum's here too..."

Straight-laced Aunty Ivy's response was not recorded.

Brad Hunter became progressively more Respectable with age. Hard to imagine from the Human Dart at the Treasury years earlier, but by the end of the decade he'd become a responsible officer of the Customs Service in Canberra. He and his wife Trish managed to join us for much of the 99 Crawl though.

At the Boardwalk on Southbank the worldly Mr. Hunter still managed to find something to pique his interest in the Men's toilet – a secure needle disposal box in "sleepy ol' Brisbane". I can't help but wonder if ten years earlier he'd have produced some chewing gum and string, and gone fishing just for the hell of it. Maturity is not always necessarily a bad thing.

Alastair adds a hazy memory of the middle stages of the Crawl. Lurch and I played splitters and went off to Gilhooley's while everyone else was boring and went to Rosies. *(Personally, I reckon they just got lost.)* Someone else was with us, a thin man with dark hair. I think he must have been a muso because he and I discussed the modal forms of music used in medieval Church liturgy. You discuss this sort of esoteric thing on pub crawls.

The patio bar at Fridays is in the shadows of the Brisbane Stock Exchange (and thus blocks away from the Stock Exchange Hotel). While there we realised we could hear the sound of Coca-Cola share prices plummeting. It could only mean one thing – Adam wasn't with us!

When we phoned to locate him we were saddened to learn his Mum was extremely sick. The number of 'family' connections on this year's Crawl only added to the poignancy. We raised our glasses quietly for a moment, and then continued on our way.

As we Crawled away from the ferry en route to the Heritage we passed a waterfront wedding in progress. Alastair recalls that it was felt proper to serenade the couple with an appropriate song. Renoir immediately launched into Skyhooks *All My Friends Are Getting Married*.

It must have been the place and time for weddings. There was another one getting ready to begin at the Heritage, but management still accepted our presence there quite calmly. So too did the bridal party, even when their Official Photographer was prevailed upon to take a shot of the bride-to-be with Alex and, of course, Eric. The only disconcerting thing, I thought, was the fact that the bride and all of her bridesmaids were younger than the Crawl.

I think Brian may have decided at some point to attempt to argue with every female on the Crawl. I can recall several contretemps with different ladies as the day progressed. At one stage Mary Therese accused Judy of depositing Brian in a pot plant on a footpath somewhere. Judy was quite adamant that he'd got into it all by himself. I didn't see it, but Judy's scenario would certainly be entirely plausible.

Someone must have made an unflattering remark to Wayne about his figure, because he took to breathing in and holding his breath a lot, trying to flatten his tummy. This lasted until his unsympathetic brother Marc said, "Don't do that – it sticks out the back."

We couldn't find a Public Bar at the Chancellors, so we sat around in the alfresco part of the restaurant. Trays of appetisers appeared from somewhere – I'm not prepared to ask how. I think someone (or two) may have been passing themselves off as waiters. The same miscreants may also have been going from table to table polishing off discarded unfinished glasses of wine, beer and spirits.

Over the unexpected nibblies Bob Clancy mentioned a little bit of

Belle Vue history – apparently some of the wrought iron lacework ended up at a house called Loa Langta in Dickson Terrace, Hamilton. I wonder if we should invite the owners on a Crawl?

Late in the event we had an *unusual* time at the Transcontinental. The bouncer on the door was being quite reasonable about letting us in, up to a point. The point was a fellow named Adam who'd joined us along our way. Adam was an almost deaf mute who worked for Castlemaine XXXX (I don't think as a taster, sadly). The poor bugger was relatively sober – more so than many of us, anyway – but made the mistake of grunting at the doorman as he passed.

Try as we might, we could *not* convince the bouncer that Adam wasn't incoherently drunk – he just couldn't talk! Frustrated, we decided on a show of solidarity and those of us already inside agreed to leave, boycotting the pub in protest.

Right at this point a coachload of line-dancers pulled up outside and disgorged its contents into the Transcontinental. I was gamely trying to exit the pub, but I was swept up in a stampede of boot-scooters in fluorescent Western costumes and silly cowboy hats. To my horror, there were people in the bar who thought that I was part of the bus-load, and someone even thrust a drink into my hand thinking I was part of their round! All very surreal…

After that, I really don't remember much of anything about the Transit Centre. I think it was on the way home from there that I discovered the restorative properties of a Subway hot 12" chicken fillet sandwich. Although by then perhaps warm wet cardboard would have seemed delicious.

.o0o.

22 2000 – HISTORY IS WRITTEN BY THE SURVIVORS

Twenty-first birthdays have great significance in our culture. They are the traditional end of youth, the beginning of responsibility, the passage into recognition of adulthood (except when it comes to ticket prices and fares, of course!). They are also used as the excuse for a bloody big party.

There is no reason why this should not equally be the case when the birthday belongs to a Half-a-Brick and his Pub Crawl.

More than the usual amount of planning went into the last Eric of the 20th Century. In recognition of the occasion we wanted to come as close as possible to the date of the very first event, so the scheduled day was September 9, 2000. Not bad, only one day out.

We were so organized that everyone on the 1999 Crawl had been given a (VERY) ADVANCE WARNING notice, which had advised the date and starting point: the Transit Centre.

As the Warning notice advised, this was chosen as it was as close as we could come to the advertised starting point of 79, the late lamented Railway Hotel.

And therein lay the biggest logistical problem for me to overcome (I'd insisted on working out the Anniversary route). I wanted to retrace our staggering steps of 79but as noted so often in previous chapters, the landscape of Brisbane's hotels and bars had changed greatly in the intervening years.

In the end, I made allowance for the likelihood that Ern, Budgie, Cleo and I had never made it up Spring Hill (no memories or photos of it, anyway) and by judicious rearrangement of the last little bit I made it possible to finish at the Story Bridge. While it wasn't on the original list, the ferry trips had become such an integral, popular part of the event that I couldn't resist including *one*. Furthermore, the National Beer Festival was on there again.

So our itinerary as we went about Reconstructing History went as follows:

Transit Centre	Transcontinental	Criterion
MacArthur's	Jimmy's On The Mall	Britannia
O'Malley's	Pig & Whistle	Rosies
Embassy	Auroras	Irish Murphy's
Lands Office	Gilhooley's	P J O'Brien's
Adrenalin	Stocky	Victory
Port Office	Heritage	Gilhooley's Downtown
Fihelly's Arms	Brisbane	Orient
Fridays	Story Bridge	

The polo shirts of the previous year had been at least a little bit effective for getting us into bars with pretensions of poshness. The 21st birthday version was in XXXX yellow, and the front featured a small depiction of Eric in a bow tie with the traditional 'key to the door' and the words *Eric's Twenty-First – More Than A Formality*. On the back was the itinerary, and a pithy quote from Benjamin Franklin suggesting that the Pub Crawl, like beer, is *proof that God loves us and wants us to be happy*. Works for me.

Eric's "coming of age" attracted a good crowd – about 35 at the Transit Centre, and some wonderful expressions of affection.

David and Val Weatherley presented a birthday card complete with a *21 Today* badge. Such consideration must be genetic, as a day earlier the postman had delivered a similar card and badge (*Be Nice To Me, It's My 21st Birthday*) all the way from England – our UK Branch, Danielle Weatherley!

Original Crawler Ern lovingly created a tasty eggless chocolate birthday cake from an "ancient family recipe", with the first ever use of his oven! With that came a present for Eric: a book of Scottish cookery. This was chosen on the basis that living with me for twenty-one years had doubtless given the Half-a-Brick a taste for things Glaswegian.

Also in the group were Marc Hunter who had deliberately avoided going to the doctor for three days rather than risk being put on antibiotics that would prevent him drinking, and his brother Wayne who gave up a corporate box seat at Willowbank raceway to attend.

It was the first Crawl as a couple for Matt Taylor and Caitlin Watters, married only a couple of weeks earlier. Not quite a honeymoon event, but close!

Geoff had come armed with an elegantly bound menu from a Chinese restaurant, the twist being that the elegant binding had been modified to resemble the infamous folder used on the TV show *This Is Your Life*. Some serious fun would be had with this as the day progressed.

The Testimonial started with rousing cheers and a birthday toast to everyone's favourite Half-a-Brick.

Amongst all the fun and frivolity though we soon had our greatest scare on a Crawl. Gregor had arrived at the Transit already feeling quite unwell. He thought it was a heavy-duty hangover, which seemed plausible enough. But his condition deteriorated rapidly, and visibly. In a photo of Lurch with Gregor and a wooden Indian outside the Criterion the carved Comanche looks healthier than Gregor.

It was clearly rather more than a hangover. Gregor's housemate Doug dashed off to find a taxi, while I tried to steer the increasingly out-of-it Iguanadon in his wake. On the George Street footpath Gregor shuffled through a little circle of backpackers sitting on a corner, trampling a couple. I placated or intimidated them, don't remember which. Either way, they sat back down and shut up. Doug had hailed a cab, and we managed to manoeuvre Gregor into the back seat. Doug stayed with him as they went to the Mater Hospital – the closest option.

A series of phone calls across the day confirmed that, as suspected, Gregor had suffered a stroke sometime during the morning. To our enormous relief he was resting comfortably and the prognosis looked pretty good.

As several people pointed out, whatever his condition Gregor would have been highly displeased had we done anything other than continue as planned. I admit to not having my mind on the Crawl until we got a reassuring phone call from Doug, though.

It was a busy day all round for Dougie: his first Eric, a mercy dash and a wait at the hospital, then in the afternoon a long-range live interview with BBC radio. The topic was, I think, what it was like to be a performance poet in Australia. Hardly a typical day to be asking on! We have a few ex-Crawlers now living in the UK, but I wonder what the average BBC listener would make of the story of Eric?

When we'd gone across the road to the Transcontinental we encountered a gentleman of, let us say, more mature vintage (he was wearing a Golden Oldies cap). Struck by the chap's resemblance to Bob Hope, Geoff entertained him with his best Mike Munro *This Is Your Life* impression, before explaining Eric's history.

The response was totally unexpected. From his pocket the Golden Oldie extracted a faded, photocopied list of Brisbane pubs of 1939 – a war years pub crawl route!

For history's sake, here is the list as written (but check out pub #1!):

On George St.:	Belle Vue, Cecil, Lands Office, Treasury, Criterion, Daniell, Lennons, Grosvenor, Majestic, Transcontinental, Railway
Albert St.:	Oriental, Warremunde's, Australian, Albert, Windsor
Edward St.:	Port Office, Victory, Exchange, Ulster, Embassy
Ann St:	Brisbane, Central Station
Margaret St.:	Grand
Elizabeth St.:	Arcadia, Theatre Royal
Charlotte St.:	Queens
Adelaide St.:	Globe, Gresham

Queen St.: York, Carlton, British Empire, Her Majesty's, Grand Central, Royal, Stock Exchange, Belfast, National, Orient

Thirty-nine pubs is testament to the staying power of the serviceman on leave, I reckon!

I'll leave it to you to compare the lists for 1939, 79 and 99 and draw your own conclusions. Some names remain in 2019, in very different guises, but precious few of the structures or even facades. And I use the word 'precious' very deliberately!

Jill Smith-Moore had a busy day planned after bringing the clan along to the Testimonial's start. It looked like we might lose Lurch early to child-minding duties, until Gill stepped up to take the job on. It was a kind gesture, and much appreciated!

When I returned to the Criterion from helping Dougie at the cab rank I was introduced to participants in the "Power Link" pub crawl. A bunch of comparative youngsters, they were a bit dismissive of the likes of Dave and I – until they looked at our list of 26 pubs alongside their five. Oops.

As Wayne and Geoff put it: "We're long haul – these guys are premature ejaculators."

MacArthur's was the renovated Lennon's. With the new look had come a positive new attitude – we were made to feel extremely welcome. I suspect we made the balance sheet for a very quiet morning look suddenly much better. Caitlin was even told that if any other bar gave us trouble we'd be welcome to come back and make up the difference!

Our reception was so positive that this became our final stop on the Cocktail Crawl of 2001 – an Eric spin-off popular as an early-on-the-calendar event for the first few years of the new Millennium.

It was at MacArthur's that Dave discovered that he *hadn't* lost his camera – only the string he'd tied it to himself with.

The lovely Mr. Weatherley was in fine form. At the Britannia Inn he stood at the door brandishing the revamped Chinese menu. When he attempted to convince two tourists of the merits of the Steamed Whole Coral Trout in Ginger and Shallots, they left.

Downstairs at the Embassy the poker machines were overshadowed by a big old-fashioned Lucky Wheel. Alastair took on the role of Bearded Barrel Girl and spun up a $1000 prize. It's a pity no tickets had been sold.

Here's an odd coincidence. When we walked into the Lands Office the race showing on Sky Channel was the Alcohol Go-Easy Cup. The winner was a horse called More Action. Neat.

Soon after that we arrived at P J O'Brien's. Over a few years there was a veritable explosion of Irish 'themed' bars all over Australia, not just in Brisbane. Globe trotting friends are confident that there are more "Traditional Irish Pubs" with all the trimmings in this country than there are back in Erin's Island.

I know it's a global phenomenon. In my own travels I've enjoyed 'Irish Bars' in Marrakesh, Beijing, Copenhagen, Paris, Greece, Estonia, Fiji, Canada and all over the US – and they're just the ones I can remember.

I suspect most of them manage to do a little better than PJ's did this day. No Guinness, no Harp, and the Kilkenny had "just run out". Inevitably, the Monty Python fans thought of the cheese shop sketch…

The incredibly short trip from PJ's to the Adrenalin Bar (they're right next door) was very important to me, because that's when Doug rang to say that Gregor was at least reasonably okay.

Not for the first time, we couldn't get into the Victory, *or* the newly renovated ultra-trendy Port Office. As noted earlier, this makes our continued acceptance at the much classier Heritage all the sweeter. Our Bundaberg visitor Meredith (her flight got her to town in time to join us at the Embassy) was at a loss to find the Ladies in the Heritage, and I'm not sure that I want to dwell too deeply on why *David* was the only person apparently able to direct her.

I was suffering quite badly from gout in 2000. After unhappy experiments with giving up beer and wine at different points, it was eventually discovered that my 'trigger' is tomatoes: fresh, sauce, even paste on pizzas or in bolognaise. That epiphany was still way in the future, and at the close of one century and into the first years of the next, I walked with the aid of a stick. On bad days, two of them. On September 9 it was only one, thankfully, leaving one hand free to clutch a glass or a Half-a-Brick, as required.

During a game of pool at the Orient it was discovered that my walking stick made a more effective cue than the 'official' implements provided by the Hotel. Certainly it was straighter. I used it quite a bit in that role subsequently, with some success. One more thing to thank Eric for, I guess.

I don't know about the rest of the survivors, but by the time I got to the Story Bridge the physical and emotional demands of the day had left me rather more worn out than usual at the end of an Eric. (No, I do *not* think I'm getting too old for this, thank you.) I'm not sure how many Crawlers wound up paying the entrance fee to the Beer Festival, but I know there were quite a few of us who elected to remain in the Public Bar and finish our celebrations there.

I think some hardy souls headed off to continue partying in the Valley. Tired and happy, I took Eric home.

.o0o.

23 LURCH'S STORY

As Jim Morrison said, what a long strange trip it's been. On the eve of Eric XXII it's time to look back on some purely personal thoughts about those many hours on the trail of just one more beer at one more pub.

The First Time is the best? Maybe. It sure stuck in my mind. The Normanby Hotel, 1986: Warm day, matching yellow shirts, bright prospect of beer all day with a big crowd of happy party people. How did it end with a drunken rant outside the Governor's residence at midnight, and a busted wrist? Come gather round children, wherever ye roam, and you'll hear a tale of drunken debauchery not seen since.

Well, actually, it really boiled down to a lack of pacing from myself. I'm still not sure what I had against the Governor that night. As for the wrist, well, there was this young woman on a bike just easing herself up the hill outside the Story Bridge, and we (I was not alone, despite rumours) were hurrying to compliment her on her fine riding style, and the taut conformation of her well-shaped thighs, and there was this gutter inconveniently placed in my path, and, well, you can join the rest of the dots*. The wrist held up well until about 6:00 am the next morning, and after a mercy dash to the Greenslopes hospital, I decided to catch the bus home to Toowoomba. Memo to self: Pace yourself, chasing women when in a drunken condition is more dangerous than when done sober.

(* Contrary to some reports, I'm sure that none of the blood that was dripping from my arm made its way into the beer glass. Maybe it's because I was quite oblivious to it until the next morning.)

Fact: this was my first and only Crawl as a single man. Jill and I got together the following Monday. I always maintain that I was in a weakened condition, but what was Jill's excuse?

So many pubs, so little time. The first beer at the Normanby tasted so good, but the pub is now stranded in the middle of the road works from Hell. St Paul's Tavern, of sainted memory, had the best beer garden. The Alliance was a great 11:30 pub, the first beers starting to bite, and perhaps a quick detour for pizza at Topolino's and the heretical bottle of wine.

The Port Office was that perfect three in the afternoon, half-shot, listen to the band sort of pub that made you want the afternoon to go on forever. This after the Story Bridge, and before the Heritage, the latter of which was always too classy for us, but always let us in, bless 'em, was the Holy Trinity of pub-crawling pubs.

Fridays turns out to be a great late afternoon pub, with margheritas a nice momentary departure from beer, beer, beer. The Orient, what a pub that was in its day, but now, sadly usually assigned to the graveyard shift of about 7:00 pm.

Because timing is all with some pubs. The best time for the Brisbane Hotel was ten years ago before they tarted it up and ruined it.

Sad the pubs that are gone: *vale* the Treasury, the Lands Office, the Majestic, the Grosvenor, the Belfast, the York, the Canberra, the National. It seems that the Belle Vue was just the beginning.

But on the upside, look at what we've gained: PJ O'Brien's, Gilhooley's Uptown and Downtown, Irish Murphy's (see a pattern here?), the Adrenalin Bar, Aurora's.

Then there are the forgotten pubs: whither the Jubilee, that fabulous beer garden, after just one time on the route? The Broadway, ditto? When will the Norman make it to the list, or will it, like the Pineapple, continue to miss out because it falls just outside an acceptable walking range? My Dream Crawl involves pubs such as the Oxley, the Brekkie Creek, the Highway Hotel and the Rocklea double act, the RE and Regatta double act, the historic pubs of Ipswich. If I win Lotto, I'll hire the minibus.

We're here for the beer. As General W T Sherman should have said, "This is a pub crawl, and a crawl means beer drinking." I get a big kick from champagne, but come crawl time it's time for a couple of gallons of brew.

I know there are some deluded souls who swear by bourbon or mother's ruin; some are willing to pay $10 for a fluted crystal goblet of Chateau Gnats Piss served rudely by a snotty waiter; I've no doubt done it myself. But beer is the way to go on a warm Brisbane day walking from pub to pub.

And if some things have declined over the last 22 years (the number of old-fashioned pubs, hell, the number of pubs), the variety and quality of beer ain't. Aside from the Queenslander's Mother's Milk (XXXX), yer standard pub is just as likely to have Cascade, Cooper's, Eumundi, Tenterfield Saddler, Toohey's Black, Guinness, Beck's, Stella, Kilkenny, Caffrey's, Theakston's Old Peculiar and Venezuelan Puma Hunter's Ale on tap.

Now while sticking to one type of beer at the footie or races is sensible and desirable, on the crawl variety is the key. Around the world in a day, you might say.

Favourite moments: watching Ben Johnson win the Olympic 100m final in the bar at the Crest; butterscotch schnapps at the Sly Fox at midnight; the time we ended early and stayed for a few hours at Dooley's; the first time we got into MacArthur's Bar without being thrown back out; pizza at Topolino's; the half-assed fruit remark; songs on the river; that time Renoir and I bellowed our way through *Wild Thing* at that Karaoke place; having raspberry lemonades with my kids at the first two pubs; all the other great times.

Doctor Luther's Prescription. I got pissed on my first crawl. Rat-arsed, shickered, molly the monk, three sheets to the wind, blotto, blind, knackered. On the skull of a Singh pirate, I swore it wouldn't happen again. And it hasn't, well, nowhere near as badly anyway.

What do I do different? Rule 1: do not drink heavy beer at every single pub; lace it with three or four lights sprinkled throughout the day. Rule 2: eat at various times throughout the day. Rule 3: bearing in mind rules

1 and 2, otherwise drink as much as you want, and stop when you've had enough. When you get home drink a lot of water and go to bed.

"It's Not Really A Crawl, Is It?" Pub crawls have had bad press, mainly because it's a pastime beloved of footy players who like to be drunk and obnoxious in as wide an area as possible. What's great about our crawl is its friendliness. We honestly just want to get loaded and have a good time. We welcome all comers; there are no rules; there are no feats of endurance; come and go as you please; bring your friends. One arrest in 20-odd years, and that was a fit-up, a couple of minor injuries. The Crawl is that strange thing, a *family* crawl. Which is probably why we've had actual families on the Crawl. Can't come? Send your kids. Or your parents.

Memories, light the corner of my mind. Thank you Babs. Now back in yer box, big-nose. As you read through Renoir's epic, you can see that the Crawl is his story as much as a story of a big free-form chaotic mobile party whose madness strikes one day every year.

With some people, it's as though they only exist for that one day, and then you don't see them for another year. But everyone's story goes on: you can see it in their faces as we gather, once again to share the drinks and the chatter and the laughter for that special one day of the year. Every year a change or two: new partners, the departure of old friends, disappearances, visitations, hallucinations. A snapshot of everyone's lives.

Will we be doing this in 20 years? I bloody hope so. If not us, let's hope it's our heirs and successors, whoever they may be.

.oOo.

24 HOW LONG CAN THIS GO ON?

It's not just about drinking, and never really was. Oh sure, that's very important. It *is* a Pub Crawl, like I said, and drinking to excess is a key identifier of such an event. But to have lasted like this one has, there has to be more to it than that. Something that makes each one Fun for so many of us.

Gill and I had lunch today with Matt Walker, his lovely wife Jenny and very young son Patrick. As we drove home, I considered the lineage.

I first met Matt on a Crawl a few years ago when he came along with Paul Kalluschke.

Paul K had first joined us some years earlier as a mate of Marc Hunter.

A couple of years before that, Marc had come along while part of a household that included Joe McLaughlin. Joe worked with me at the time, and liked the sound of the earlier Pub Crawls that I'd described.

Friends of friends, becoming friends themselves. A network that has evolved, and continues to do so, over more than two decades. Persisting irrespective of differences in our backgrounds, distances between our homes – some of us, as Lurch noted, only see each other on this one day of the year and yet seem to pick up conversations where we left off.

New faces appear every year. Some don't last, but others find that there's something about the camaraderie of an Eric that particularly appeals to them. They keep coming back, becoming part of our history.

I believe we'll progressively see more Crawlers who are younger than the Crawl itself.

Friends and colleagues. Second generation starters. I hope that in my dotage my bathchair may be pushed around an Eric route by Patrick, or Lurch's kids – the offspring of any of my friends who've seen what we do every year and decide that they want to be part of it, too.

A thought disconcerts me. This is how religions start, isn't it? (And I've always considered 'religion' the worst thing that ever happened to God.) Eric an icon – me as the first Pope of Pub Crawling? Naah, I don't think so.

To paraphrase what I said back in 1979: it isn't a congregation, it's just a fun event. Long may it remain so!

On behalf of Eric and I – we've had a great time, thank you and goodnight...

.o0o.

PART TWO: THE NEXT MILLENNIUM

25 NEW THINGS

You might think the second twenty years would be easier to recollect, being more recent, eh?

Sadly, it doesn't work that way. My memory is not one of those that has improved with age. Although admittedly, the problem is much as Karl remarked so long ago – I'm good with moments, it's years I struggle with.

So some of what follows may be out of sequence. I don't think any of it is just plain wrong. I've collated notes, photos, emails, whatever I could find. Oddly, the more recent events have given me most trouble.

Older photographs have timestamps and datestamps from when they were taken or printed. Digital technology has robbed me of some of those clues, as the dates I've got refer to when the pictures were loaded onto this particular machine – not necessarily the date of capture.

Likewise some documents didn't make it onto my current buzz-box, lost over successive upgrades and replacements.

The second half of Eric's existence (as an entity separate from the late, lamented Belle Vue) has been a time of change, globally and personally. The pace of that change has been extraordinary, yet that makes the 'anchor' of a history like this valuable. When I want to remember what life was like before emails and mobile phones – well, here it is. 'Wet' photocopiers, invitations sent by mail, concerned calls from public phones, all there in Part One.

As to the personal changes, well, it's said that change is a constant. Back in 2001 Lurch observed that this book is as much my history as Eric's, and I suppose that's inevitable. So yes, you get some of my rollercoaster ride, but I hope you also get some sense of some of the other characters who've come along on this wacky journey over the years.

The mid-to-late 00s brought a bunch of new people on board, some of whom have become integral to the annual Crawl. There's a fair case to say some helped keep it going when I wasn't sure I was up to it. They know who they are and, I hope, know how grateful I am.

So, as my Grade 12 History teacher Cecil Munns used to say: "Right, let's make a start..."

.o0o.

26 2001 – A BRICK'S ODYSSEY

The year itself made the theme for the Crawl just too easy. Arthur C. Clarke's novel, and Stanley Kubrick's movie, had made '2001' an inseparable segue into 'A Space Odyssey', or something resembling it.

So the year's polo shirt had an astronaut, stars, a galactically-floating Half-a-Brick, and the completely unrelated motto: Insanity: a statement, not a plea

Not quite sure now why that was chosen. Probably some external observer had told us we're all mad.

On the back was a new Latin motto, courtesy of Gregor: ERIC erit in orbe ultima* (Eric will outlast all other powers). There was also the itinerary, styled after the opening credits of Star Wars.

Said itinerary was a clever one planned by Ian McLeod. It was 'scientifically designed' to avoid any hill climbs, and so earned the subtitle "The Downhill Run". It's a pity a few pubs' failure to open as expected blew the plan out of the water once or twice, but still – worth preserving the list:

Spring Hill Tavern	Spring Hill Hotel	Alliance
Bonaparte's	Shamrock	Latin
Royal George	O'Kelly's	Orient
Brisbane	Fihelly's Arms	Rosies
Embassy	Stockie	Victory
Heritage	Story Bridge	Plough
Clarence Corner	Morrison	Railway
Gabba	Broadway	

So, on August 25 we got together at the Spring Hill Tavern (not Hotel).

114

The venue formerly called the Grand Chancellor, on the site of the old City View.

There were several new faces, as usual, and the return of a familiar face from too long back – Michael Perisic. A very welcome return!

We even had a 'merchandise table' courtesy of Iain Moore – he and Wendy were operating a new business selling various promotional wares, and we were a good opportunity for them to try out some of their new equipment. There were badges, plastic cups, stubby holders, and even luminescent alien masks (as befitting the 2001 theme), all emblazoned with a very familiar likeness and of course the words *I'm A Close Personal Friend Of ERIC.*

Next stop was the Spring Hill Hotel (not Tavern). This used to be the Leichhardt in years gone by, so neither of the two squabbling venues could lay truthful claim to being 'original'. First of two latecomers at best.

For reasons long forgotten the pub was having a sale of sports equipment and paraphernalia. Leftovers from a charity function perhaps? Certainly it's the sort of thing our charity did in later years. (More of that in subsequent chapters – be patient.) The two purchases I recall, and I don't think either was especially pricey, were Iain Moore buying a bagful of golf clubs and Matt Walker buying a shirt.

Both buys had more than a touch of quirkiness about them. I don't recall Iain showing any interest in playing golf, before or since. I may be doing him a disservice, but I've always believed cycling to be his thing, since we gave up playing football together many moons ago. (Occasional Crawler Rosco is fond of reminding me, "You like your life – don't ruin it by taking up golf." He is of course tragically addicted to the game himself.)

The shirt that Matt bought was an Aussie one-day cricket shirt, framed and autographed by its original wearer, wicket-keeper Ian Healy. Why I suspect it hadn't sold at auction was that the autograph very clearly and specifically said, "*To Patrick, regards Ian Healy*".

Presumably there'd been no-one at the auction named Patrick. Fortunately, that's the name of Matt's son. Too young at the time to appreciate it, but once he was old enough to understand the history of the game, I'm sure he was impressed.

It wasn't long before Iain lugged his new purchases home, though not before he and Lurch alarmed other bar patrons with a few practice swings. Given the disparity of height between the two blokes, I'm sure one or other would have been at a serious disadvantage. Matt, on the other hand, carried his new acquisition around for much if not all of the day, I think. He must have been careful with the package, whatever his own condition, because it got home safely.

Bonaparte's I seem to recall was struggling for business by then. In an attempt to attract custom they'd reduced the amount of clothing that the bar staff wore. I think there was also a raffle going on that we stayed for – meat trays? Chooks? Free beer? Someone among us may even have won one, then either sold or gave away the prize.

As we walked, Paul Kalluschke recorded events on a strange little disposable camera he'd found, decorated with more cosmic artwork to celebrate the year 2001. Passing an op shop in Brunswick Street, he dashed inside and re-emerged soon after in his new guise. Sporting hard hat and overalls, no, not Bob The Builder (sorry kiddies), he'd transformed into Bob The Boozer! Altogether now: "Can we drink it? Yes we can!" Okay, maybe you had to be there.

Marc also changed outfits a couple of times over the course of the day. At one point in the Valley he was wearing what was introduced as his late grandfather's suit – although I don't think that it really was "the one he was buried in". Whatever the origin, its previous owner was clearly a slighter figure than Marc who described the outfit as being "so tight that if I sneeze my right nut will fly out my nose".

Must be my sense of humour – that one line still remains one of the funniest moments I can recall on any Eric.

I think that O'Kelly's was the current name for a nice old pub on

Wickham Street that has had a number of identities since opening as the Prince Consort in the 1888. I think, too, that it was there that a very obliging publican by the name of Les Pullos welcomed us by laying on some nibblies, and delivering a fine speech in which he introduced Eric to his regular patrons. (If I've got the pub wrong, my sincere apologies to Les who did very well by us, wherever we were!)

There was a more substantial than usual contingent of ATO staff, past and current, and most of us assembled for a photo on the way to the Story Bridge; there was me, Lurch, Alastair, Craig Wyrill, Lynne Hall, Ron Vallance, Ben Lurje, and Matt Mitchell. Plus ex-ATO Karl, who'd made the trip up from Sydney this time.

The Story Bridge has another significance. It was around this time that several of us first encountered PK Tate running a trivia competition in the Bombshelter Bar, filling in for the usual host. The positive impression was mutual – I have a very clear recollection of the entire audience erupting into a singalong of the theme from *The Greatest American Hero* – one of PK's favourites, probably led by Lurch and I. Other people might have stopped at the chorus, but not us.

> Believe it or not,
> I'm walkin' on air,
> I never thought I could feel so free;
> Flyin' away on a wing and a pray'r,
> Who could it be?
> Believe it or not, it's just me.

The friendship with PK continued to grow at the Brunswick Hotel with a regular trivia team ("The Loud Shirts") made up of Pub Crawlers Gill, Judy, Lurch, Adam, Gregor, Craig and me. Lunchtime quizzes at the Pig & Whistle really deepened the mateship into one that became very important a few years later. I'll get to that. Back to 2001...

The closure of the Victoria Bridge, and more critically the huge crowds that descended on Southbank due to the fireworks spectacular Skyfire complicated matters on Ian's carefully mapped route. Credit to everyone for displaying their flexibility – no surprises there!

We missed the south side completely, and added a run along the top end of town that included the newly-reopened Grosvenor, at last shedding its Mac-prefix. It wasn't the pub it used to be, other than its façade. But it did serve wine in very, very large glasses, to Sharon's delight.

Some of the quicker drinkers were able to get over the Vic Bridge before it was closed to pedestrian traffic. Others of us, unaware that was even a prospect, found ourselves temporarily stuck. Fortunately, there was another bar to linger in.

I think we spent a while at the Crest. Those who wanted could stand outside and watch the pretty lights in the sky. Others settled into some very comfortable lounges and got Mellow.

After the pyrotechnics were done we managed to get across the bridge for a finish, not inappropriately, at the Terminus. Some of that earlier group were still there waiting, and some had wandered off into the night seeking other bars. Perhaps even those missed previously in the day.

At least four of the glowing 'little green man' masks had made it to the end. Cathy, Gregor, Ian and I are wearing them in the final photo, with Sandra looking on amused. I think.

Strangely enough, several days later, I was in hospital having some of my insides removed. I don't remember the details, but I'm pretty sure it was coincidence…

.oOo.

27 2002 – AN ODYSSEY OF HOMERIC PROPORTIONS

The surgeon's knife was out again in June of 2002, as Gill endured her first cancer surgery. To be honest, as bad as it was, the surgery was less traumatic for her than the subsequent chemotherapy. I will always remember how distraught she was the day I had to shave off the last remnants of her beautiful hair.

Yes, it eventually grew back, but she was – we were, so distressed that I've never been able to appreciate the light-hearted tone of the Shave For A Cure events. Raise awareness, raise funds sure, but don't make a joke of it. But I'm probably over-sensitive.

In any case, by the time we were planning for the next Eric a lift in spirits really was called for. Somehow I (or someone) thought of what became my favourite Eric polo shirt.

Homer Simpson adorns the front, his finger in a foamy beer glass, smiling happily with the word balloon "mmm... **pub crawl...**" and Eric on the bar beside him.

On the back, Bart is writing his lines on the blackboard, with those lines being the itinerary. It also included the words to the Simpsons' drinking song (you'll know the tune):
        DOUGH – the stuff that buys my beer
        RAY – the guy that sells me beer
        ME – the guy who drinks the beer
        FAR – the distance to my beer
        SO – I think I'll have a beer
        LA – la la la la la beer
        TEA – no thanks, I'm drinking beer
        That will bring us back to
        D'OH!!!

Yes, I did write to Matt Groening and get permission, well in advance. The letter itself is, sadly, one of the things that disappeared in a change of computer. Or address, or something.

Anyway, by October 12 the shirts were ready, and so were we. The route was:

Dooleys	Empire	Royal George
Elephant & Wheelbarrow	Wickham	Jubilee
Shamrock	Bonapartes	Alliance
Bookies	Orient	Macarthurs
Fridays	Story Bridge	Stamford
Port Office	Victory	Stockie
Embassy	Downunder	Berkleys
Fihellys Arms	Crest	Grosvenor
Criterion	Terminus	Plough Inn

O'Kelly's had changed identities again, and was now the Elephant & Wheelbarrow, a wonderfully old-fashioned name for an old pub, even if it was in the process of remodeling itself rather 'modernly'. I wonder if perhaps there was an issue over the name clashing with 'Kelly's' over in South Brisbane, but then that place also had some identity crises before eventually closing its doors.

Our television screens at the time were awash with ads for a laundry product called NapiSan. It was touted by an earnest fellow brandishing a clipboard and waving his microphone under the noses of people in the street, or their back yards, or the laundry. Those ads were the inspiration for Geoff taking over Dave's *This Is Your Life* schtick, and randomly 'interviewing' people on the street as we travelled.

'On the street' literally sometimes, as he approached cars stopped at traffic lights to quiz drivers and passengers on their laundry habits, and to tell them about Eric. The most memorable was at the lights outside the Jubilee, where it chanced that the car he'd targeted was an unmarked police car. The uniformed officers were too bemused to do anything – either arrest Geoff or immediately drive away when he asked about how they kept their shirts so nice and blue. They actually missed a turn of the lights (fortunately there was nobody queued behind them) before eventually driving away shaking their heads.

As ever, we sang our way over to the Story Bridge and back, but this year our 'song list' was expanded by a ditty composed by Alastair's two sons, Iain and Bernard. To the tune of the jingoistic – sorry, *patriotic* TV jingle '*We Are Australian*', it went like this (thank you, young gentlemen):

> We aren't young
> But we are merry, And to all your pubs we come,
> We like our beer,
> Our wine, our sherry,
> I want, you want
> We want another one.

There was another 'moment' with Security at the Stock Exchange late in the afternoon. The bouncer just coming on duty decided that my two walking sticks (it was a bad gout day) were offensive weapons, and I wasn't to be allowed in. I'd had just enough gin, and was in just enough pain, to get a bit belligerent about this, and was seriously considering demonstrating just how offensively the canes could be employed.

Someone, possibly Lurch and Sharon, diplomatically stepped in and steered me away. Away, around the corner, and in through the entrance that the Security staff hadn't yet arrived at. Left the same way too, nodding politely to my erstwhile adversary as I rounded the corner and passed.

We didn't get past the front entrance of the Downunder Bar – a haven for out-of-towners, mostly foreign backpackers. The first few Crawlers to arrive there were deemed to be "too old" to be admitted, and the rest, arriving soon after, decided the place didn't deserve our dollars. Bloody cheek. "Too old." Apparently we wouldn't fit the youthful ambience they were nurturing. Or maybe they thought, at our age we might be disturbed enough by something going on in there to blow the whistle to some authority. Shows how little they knew about the

Friends of Eric. "Too old." Harrumph.

Berkleys was the elegant bar attached to the foyer of an up-market hotel opposite Central Station. It had turned up on one of the cocktail crawls we'd indulged in for a while (the "Frocked-Up Pub Crawls"). Given the refined tone of the place, I was much impressed at how welcome we were made to feel. Shades of the Heritage. There was a smooth, amiable and very efficient barman on duty. My enduring memory is of him deftly and diplomatically removing a cigarette from the lips of a rather worse-for-the-day young lady who was with us (possibly a tag-along – we sometimes collect them), explaining that there was no smoking in the bar, and handing her the glass of wine she'd ordered. I think he even returned it, still unlit, as she left.

I might not recall details of the ending, but I do know that the day was a good boost to the spirits (as well as spirit sales in a lot of venues). Good to have friends.

.o0o.

28 2003 - CHALLENGING

 While travelling in Europe Judy had sent Gill and I a postcard we really liked. (Y'see kids, back in those days we sent postcards, not e-mails – old technology.) It showed two blokes at a sidewalk café in Paris, mopping their intimidated brows as they contemplate a pair of very, VERY large beer glasses. Put it like this: each has the shape of a brandy balloon and the proportions of a weather balloon.

 It only took a little effort to put Eric on the table alongside the glass, and add the inscription: *Be Challenged!* And presto: there was the front of the t-shirt.

 I have a photo of Matt and Caitlin's young son Daniel, not yet three, in his own kid-sized version of the t-shirt.

 There had been some concerns expressed by some Crawlers that the number of new bars and name changes were making it hard to keep track of the annual itinerary. Changing the route every year makes for excellent and interesting variety (as well as being something of a necessity with Brisbane's rapidly evolving barscape) but if you're not in or around the CBD all the time, yes, it can be a bit bewildering.

 The solution that year was to print a map on the back of the shirt. It meant that geographically challenged folk could simply follow the directions on the back of someone walking ahead of them. Presuming they knew the streets of Brisbane. And that they weren't at the head of the procession themselves, and hopelessly lost... Still, it was a good theory!

 The 13th of September saw a good crowd assemble in the Valley, complete with the musical accompaniment of Ern on the ukulele!

I'm still trying to locate the map, but I do have photographic evidence of the following, in order:

    Elephant & Wheelbarrow   Wickham   Shamrock
    Bonaparte's   St Pauls   Sportsman
    Spring Hill Hotel   Spring Hill Tavern   Cheers
    Fihelly's Arms   Berkley's   Downunder
    Pig & Whistle Riverside   Port Office   Heritage
    Plough

I have more than a sneaking suspicion that St. Paul's was closed. The building looks distinctly unopen in the picture, with a couple of people sauntering past, uninterested. It also looks very like the beautiful beer garden has been roofed, walled in, and turned into "Halos Restaurant". Playing on the *Saint* Paul's name, I suppose. It looks quite unencumbered by customers, and thoroughly unblessed.

Cheers was the new identity of the International, a Spring Hill pub that had sometimes been on the fringe of an Eric, just slightly out of the way enough (down a hill of enough steepness to bother the lazy) to sometimes be omitted. Very much in its favour though, as years passed, was the fact that it developed one of the best and most interesting ranges of tap beers in the city.

While the name was clearly pinched from the TV series ("you wanna be where everybody knows your name…") I don't believe it was actually a part of the real Cheers franchise. I've been to both of the Boston bars officially bearing the name, including the original one where the filming was done, and the Spring Hill version had none of the merchandise and memorabilia that they do. And I can't imagine an owner or publican failing to make money like that if it was legally possible!

Almost a shame really. They make great t-shirts. This was the show that gave us such memorable lines as:
    "Whatcha up to, Norm?"
    "My ideal weight, if I was eleven feet tall."

It was another Crawl with a substantial ATO presence. Staffers past and present included Rowdy Allkin, Filthy Foley, Tony Anstis, Rhys Lewis, Ron Vallance, Terry McFarland, Lurch, Rosco, Alastair, Megan, Lynne, Renoir, and Gill.

The 'Be Challenged' theme was risen to by Gill, back on her feet, sporting a headful of new curly locks. Sometimes post-chemo re-growth turns out quite different to the lost hair, apparently. While she was careful with what she drank, plenty of water interspersed with the wine, she defiantly lasted for the entire Crawl.

There was still a substantial crew at the Plough when the Crawl finished – one of the best 'survival' rates for a long time, I think. I can vouch for Gill, Wayne, Tony, Gregor, Alastair, Ian, Eleanor, Megan, and a few faces that I recognise but can't put names to. Also with us at the end was Ern, who'd had the sense to protect his sometimes-fragile health by leaving us as we headed up Spring Hill, then coming back (*sans* ukulele, unfortunately but probably wisely) to wait for us at the 'finishing post'.

.o0o.

29 2004 – A STUDY IN SILVER

2004, the 25th anniversary Crawl! So we went with the Silver Jubilee theme of course.

The t-shirts were grey – a shade as close to silver as I could manage, with dark blue sleeves. I couldn't get the royal blue that I wanted.

On the front was a painstakingly drawn rendition of the Queen's silver jubilee 50c piece, (all those little crowns were a pest to draw!) with Eric as the centrepiece. The same design was used for the badges that Iain and Wendy produced.

The back was adorned with a somewhat retouched picture of said monarch. Retouched by having Eric on her lap, an empty beer glass on the couch beside her, an Official Brick Carrier's Nose on her face, and her identity 'obscured' by one of those white rectangles over her eyes that the papers use for 'anonymity' that doesn't fool anyone. Oh, and a word balloon: "We are amused…" – Betty W., somewhere in England.

It was Sharon's favourite Eric t-shirt, and she still wears it on appropriate occasions.
I don't think she has royalist sympathies – just likes the design.

Reproduced here, the text of the Official Invitation that went out, sticking with the theme:

> Hear Ye! Here Ye!
>
> It being 25 years since the lamentable demolition of the Belle Vue Hotel led to the initiation of Eric The Half-A-Brick, your presence is herebyrequested at his Silver Jubilee Testimonial Pub Crawl.
>
> The date will be Saturday September 18.

Commencement will be at 10.00am at the Royal George (seems apt) in Brunswick Street, Fortitude Valley. (Breakfast available beforehand).

Thereafter the OBE (Order of Brick Entry) will be:

Royal George	Deck Bar	Elephant & Wheelbarrow
Wickham	Jubilee	Shamrock
Alliance	St Pauls	Bookmakers Club
Tank	Pig & Whistle	Fridays
Story Bridge	Stamford Heritage	Port Office
Brussels Beer Cafe	Embassy	Adrenalin
P J O'Brien's	Gilhooley's	Aurora's
Irish Murphy's	Macarthurs	Terminus
Plough Inn		

For those who think we seem to be walking past some options: Bonaparte's and City Rowers are currently closed for renovations - if they're open again by 18/9 that's a bonus. The Victory and Stock Exchange are being ignored for past indiscretions of the Security Staff variety. More forgiving Crawlers are welcome to take their own chances there.

Some of the route in hindsight seems odd to me, but I'm sure we made it work somehow.

I got a good RSVP from Karl, who couldn't escape Sydney that weekend: I will certainly have a Pub Crawl on Saturday. It might only be a crawl between the gin fridge, the tonic fridge and the sofa, but I will crawl.

Young Daniel Taylor, having appeared in a photograph in 2003, now appeared in person at the first pub or two, again sporting his own kid-sized t-shirt. (In white, as I couldn't get the grey in miniature. Still, it's the thought that counts.)

Adding a touch of sartorial elegance (or something), Ian McLeod, Paul K and I all wore suit coats for the occasion. Royal formality, perhaps?

Gill didn't do the whole Crawl this time – I think she'd proved a point to herself the year before, but joined us for a fair chunk of the day.

Also returning for an all-too-rare visit were Lyola and Pete, or as more usually known, Bruce and Bruce. It's a Monty Python reference, again, and if I have to explain it then I'm sorry, you need to take a bit of responsibility for your own education. Maybe the University of Wooloomooloo would be appropriate.

I have some memory of feeling a bit weary late in the afternoon, and some of us taking time out to play pool at Aurora's, which was also a brewery making its own interesting wares.

There's also an unpleasant feeling that this was the year that a particularly unpleasant bouncer gave us grief at the Irish bar on George Street that had for many years been the Treasury Tavern and briefly pinched the name of the old Lands Office. It had large windows opening onto Elizabeth Street, and a few of us had stopped as we walked to chat to Crawlers already inside and drinking at the counter under the window.

It's *possible* that someone handed a glass out, saying "Try this" before we went inside. No-one ever admitted to doing that, or seeing it though. But the belligerent bouncer stormed up to us demanding that we "get the hell away from there". Next thing we knew, he'd sized up who was the frailest looking amongst us – the lean grey-haired figure of Alastair – and decked him. I saw Alastair go down and the proverbial red mist descended. All that prevented what would have been the first real brawl on a Crawl was the good sense and strength of Megan's boyfriend of the time. I wish I could remember the burly diplomat's name. He was a big lad though, and got me in a bearhug from behind. I think the bouncer advanced a pace, thinking he had an ally, but was stared down.

"We're going in to join our friends for a drink. Back off. Back off now."

Said quietly, but with a great deal of force and conviction. He backed off. We went in, picking up Alastair and dusting him off as we did so.

Fortunately he'd been inebriated enough to not be damaged, or at least not feel any pain. In truth, he literally didn't know what hit him. We left after a round of drinks, via a different door, with me still fuming. It turned out to be a small turning point in Eric history.

There were three interesting new additions to the itinerary. The Bookmakers Club was a regular haunt of a few of the Tax folk, notably yours truly. Halfway along Wharf Street, it was a welcoming place, unlike some of Brisbane's theoretically exclusive Clubs, and it's much missed.

The Tank Hotel on Queen Street was alleged to take its name from being on the site of colonial Brisbane's first water tank, situated in a cattle paddock between the creek (now Creek Street) and the cart track leading down to the wharf (now Wharf Street). I think it was owned (not operated) by a couple of prominent sporting types – Rugby Union players if a faint memory is correct. In a few years time it would become very important to many Crawlers, but for now it was a slightly quirky little place that felt a bit more like a licensed TAB than a pub.

And then there was the Brussels – a.k.a. the Belgian Beer Café. This was a particular favourite for Lurch, Alastair and me. An indulgence for days when our wallets could keep pace with our tastes, as the name implies it was a bar that specialised in the usually excellent, sometimes extraordinary beers of Belgium.

They sold Stella Artois, too, but I think many Belgians hold Stella in the same regard as many Aussies hold Fosters. It's something for the tourists to drink, to keep them from depleting our stocks of the *good* stuff. There were fruit beers, including the delightfully appropriate BelleVue range (their raspberry beer remains a favourite when I can find it). If sweetness wasn't your thing there were gems like the whiskey-laced Gouden Carolus. For those who wanted to prove their toughness, there was what was claimed to be the 'world's strongest beer' – one of the Bush range. (I wasn't a fan. I reckon they'd sacrificed flavour for strength.)

While Eric's annual event is all about commemorating a lost pub, and many more that have gone over the years, it is also worth recognising that there have been new venues appear, some of which have proved very worthwhile. I'm not convinced that any will last anything like a hundred years, though.

.o0o.

30 2005 - SOMETHING WICKED THIS WAY CRAWLS...

In February of 2005 the Channel Ten News ran a story on the Belle Vue.

> The graceful old hotel was once home to Katharine Hepburn and "anyone who was anyone" stayed there.
>
> The State government had owned it for 12 years. They let it get run down - and then they pulled it down. At the orders of the Premier Joh Bjelke Petersen.
>
> Today, historians still wonder what life would be like if the Belle Vue had survived. But in some ways - much of it did. Its treasures were stripped and sold off at auction.

The story suggested that much of what was sold went to George Deen, one of the brothers driving the demolition equipment. It was said that he'd bought much of the ornate ironwork from the façade, and then 'stored' it under the Story Bridge, from where, George said, much of it was stolen.

The story finished with a plea from the reporter.

> So if you know who has the Belle Vue's treasures, local historians would like to know. Only 10% of the Belle Vue's artifacts made it to that auction. The rest are still out there somewhere!

Well, I know where *one* piece of Belle Vue history is, and George Deen is *not* getting his hands on it!

That one piece fronted up for his annual outing on September 10. It was a very different route to the usual, completely avoiding the CBD of Brisbane. I'm sure there was a good reason for that, or maybe we really just wanted a bit of variety. That would be a good reason.

Paddington Tavern	Caxton	Normanby
Cheers	Grand Chancellor	Spring Hill
Sportsman	Alliance	St Pauls
Metro On Gibbs	Shamrock	Elephant & Wheelbarrow
Royal George	Empire	Mustangs
Dooley's		

A very restrained sixteen pubs. I think we'd finally started to realise that the later stages of a long Crawl were becoming just too much of a hassle with overzealous Security staff. Most of us were up for the drinking, but not up for the arguments and potential fights. The incident on Elizabeth street in 2004 was the final straw. We were there to enjoy ourselves, not risk being belted, or being goaded into starting a blue.

In some ways I suppose that realization ran counter to an inscription from the 2005 'Invitation' that went out: "Maturing" is something best left to good red wines, term deposits, and certain cheeses.

That line didn't make it onto the t-shirt. In fact, this year was the only time I put myself into the shirt design – a very grumpy old version of me it was, too. A top-hatted version of my 'Truckle the Uncivil' character from *Interesting Times*, with cane and a t-shirt that read 'I'm still a close personal friend of Eric'.

Truckle was a geriatric barbarian, one of the Silver Horde, wonderful comic creations from the masterful Terry Pratchett. Several of the Crawlers over the years became involved in the Brisbane Arts Theatre's annual productions of plays adapted from Terry's *Discworld* novels.

The top hat and cane were representative of what I'd been wearing in 2004, and the words "Something wicked this way CRAWLS" indicate that the memory of that bloody bouncer was still all too clear in my mind.

To the art was added the words: Growing older is largely inescapable. Growing wiser, thankfully, is not.

And yet, honestly, it seems we had. Or I had, a bit at least. It was a trouble-free Crawl, that much I know.

The Paddo was a starting pub that had long been talked about – I think Lurch was a particular promoter of the idea, and indeed may even have been the one responsible for planning the route.

That's a vital task that is too often under-rated and underappreciated. It is sometimes, not always, accomplished by a 'trial run' reconnaissance to check on what bars exist, and are open at what time. It's annoying how many places don't open until later on a Saturday, and an unplanned itinerary could all too often lead to standing forlornly in front of a door that wasn't due to open for another two hours.

For Lurch's sake, I'd like to say that the Paddo proved itself worthy of the honour, but I don't remember us being made especially welcome. Not *unwelcome*, just perhaps a bit inconvenient for bar staff who'd wanted a quiet morning. Maybe they had their own hangovers to nurse. The biggest problem was that public transport to Paddington was rather more awkward than to the city, or South Brisbane or the Valley, mainly because there's no convenient railway station nearby. If we ever started there again, I don't remember it. Then again, there's quite a bit about some subsequent years that I don't remember...

Ian McLeod remembers being one of the first to arrive at St. Paul's Tavern (just ahead of a loud and, let's say *obvious* group) to a less than warm reception from the bar manager.

The fellow in question apparently rolled his eyes, looked to the heavens and muttered all-too-audibly, "Oh God, is it *that* time of year again?"

I reckon he took our money though.

.o0o.

31 2006 – THE SOUTH SHALL RISE AGAIN

After a few years of Fortitude Valley starts, then the Paddington 'experiment', it was thought that a return to the Other side of the river was in order. *So* in order that eight of the sixteen bars on the route were on the south side of the river!

Referencing the colours of The South in the American Civil War, the shirts for the year were in Confederate grey.

There was a pocket-sized logo on the front of the shirt: Eric against a background of a flag that Robbo had designed for me years earlier. The flag was an amalgam of the Scottish saltire and the Eureka flag, capturing my family history and political/historical leanings. Technically meaningless to anyone else, but it looked suitably reminiscent of the old Confederate flag to go with the words circling the image: The SOUTH shall rise again! – 27th Eric The Half A Brick Testimonial PUB CRAWL.

It was another Downhill Run, as noted on the back with the itinerary.

Marc & Sharon planned the route:
> The idea was that there were no hills involved, it has a mix of old/new/theme pubs and it ends in the mall where we can find somewhere to eat after.

Also on the back of the shirt was the quote "A quart of ale is a dish for a king!" from Shakespeare's The Winter's Tale. Shakespeare was on my mind, as I'd been working on the rock opera version of the Bard's Scottish Play at QPAC.

That also explained our starting point, as that particular venue was a major sponsor of the show, and a regular gathering place post-rehearsal. (My mother was of course astonished that people were paying to hear me sing. And I was never able to sneak *Gilligan's Island* into the show.) But I felt sufficiently indebted to the pub to lobby for it to be #1 of the year's sixteen.

Chalk	Morrison	Clarence
Ship Inn	Boardwalk	Plough
Greystones	Fox	Criterion
CBD	Brewhouse	Gilhooley's
Union Jack's	Stock Exchange	Victory
Stamford Heritage		

The Chalk was an interesting pub in its own right anyway. It was on the site of the old Railway Hotel (if memory serves me correctly), but was a modern confection of glass and stainless steel. Very welcoming, though – owned by a consortium of sportsmen, including, I think, Ian Healy whose shirt Matt had bought years earlier. I don't remember ever seeing any of them there though – certainly not on Pub Crawl Day.

The Brewhouse was the new identity of Auroras. I don't think much had changed though. The pool tables were still popular, and the beers they produced in-house were still tasty and popular.

Union Jack's was a British 'themed bar', and in its early days at least had a terrific selection of beers from all over the UK not commonly found in this country. It was where I first found Titanic – one of the best stouts I ever encountered. The excellent Wychwood range was available, and several Irish beers outside the usual selections like Guinness and Kilkenny.

To compound the danger to one's waistline there, next door was a newly opened doughnut shop that had an array of ridiculously sweet confections: iced in a dozen flavours, filled with cream, custard, jam, and even Turkish delight! That latter won me – I think I knocked off a box of six of them with a pint of stout and called that lunch.

And yet, this is the most difficult of all Pub Crawls for me to reflect upon. Not because we didn't enjoy ourselves, or because there was any lack of goodwill amongst us. Far from it.

I mentioned above that I was working on the rock opera of the Scottish play at the time. Yes, I'm superstitious enough now to not call it by name, and I reckon I've good reason. The last time I'd been in a version of that play had been 2002, when Gill was first diagnosed with cancer. In 2006 it happened again. Relapse, they call it.

The Crawl was on the 14th of October 2006. Gill was in hospital over at Greenslopes, awaiting more surgery. At the Clarence Corner Hotel everyone chipped in to buy a huge bouquet from the florist at the Mater Hospital. I think there was so much collected that we bought two. I jumped into a taxi and dashed over to deliver them, together with a card and lots of hugs from everyone there.

I think I rejoined the Crawl at the Fox, but I'm not really sure. I know I did rejoin, though, bearing Gill's love and best wishes, and her avowed intent to be back with everyone next year.

Fortunately for the high spirits of everyone on that October day we didn't know what lay just ahead. Those flowers arrived at Gill's bedside a little more than a month before she died, on November 19.

.o0o.

32 2007 – AN ACT OF CHARITY

There's a lot of the next year or two (or more) that's a blur to me. I gave up work – never really fitted in the Public Service anyway – and spent a lot of time in front of the television, watching old movies and series. Every episode of Doctor Who, for instance.

Within weeks of Gill's death, my mother took sick, went from the house we'd all shared into hospital for a few months, and from there to an Aged Care Home, where she stayed, bedridden, for a few more years.

What kept me from a totally self-destructive spiral was the love and support of my friends. The Close Personal Friends of Eric – my Pub Crawl family.

Several years earlier I'd read a cheery book of anecdotes called *Old Bastards I Have Met*, written by a bloke named Sam Weller. Inspired by it, I'd joined the Australasian Order of Old Bastards, a charity founded in 1968 that did a lot of good, and didn't take itself at all seriously.

At Gill's memorial service, I'd asked that instead of spending money on flowers, people could make a donation to the Gallipoli Medical Research Foundation. Their work on cancer might well have helped Gill if her relapse had been caught earlier.

PK Tate, our favourite trivia host, was also a card-carrying Old Bastard. After the service he and I contemplated the substantial sum of money that had been donated, and decided it was time for a Brisbane branch of the AOOB. It took a couple of months to get organized, but in March **Gill's Old Bastards** became an active reality. *For good times and doing some good* was the motto.

The Tank Hotel was GOBs' home base. From the earliest days, money was raised via meat trays and quiz nights. Then we thought of the Walk Against Thirst.

It's the only Pub Crawl in Australia that's older than our Eric event. Just. It started on ANZAC Day in 1978, and has followed the same route around the Rocks in Sydney every year since. At every pub a collection tin is passed around, and every year a charity is chosen to receive the largesse of the ANZAC Day drinkers. "What a good idea!" we thought.

So the September 15 Crawl was the first one where we toted around both Eric AND a collection tin, gathering change as we went.

Separate emails went out to members of Gill's Old Bastards, and past Crawlers who'd yet to join the august Order, with the only substantial differences being a history of Eric for OBs who'd not yet met him, and alternatively a brief history of the AOOB, and an encouragement to spend $15 on a Life Membership. (Many did.)

We stayed with the south side start but added a new wrinkle in the middle – a carefully planned wrinkle:

Burke's Red Brick	Clarence Corner	Morrison
Ship Inn	Plough Inn…	

Then catch a Citycat from SouthBank Jetty 2 (nearest to the Plough towards Vic bridge)

Ferry times: 11.50 12.04 12.17 12.44 12.58

Arr. Toowong: 12.01 12.15 12.28 12.55 1.09

    Regatta…

Citycat times: 12.29 12.43 12.56 1.23 1.37

Arr. North Quay: 12.36 12.50 1.03 1.30 1.44

Lennons Bar	Brewhouse	Gilhooley's
Union Jacks	Stock Exchange	Victory

Belgian Beer Café   Heritage   Pig & Whistle Tank

There was no official Crawl t-shirt this year, but it was the first appearance of the GOBs polo shirts which became common attire for several years. They were teal – one of Gill's favourite colours – with the GOBs logo and the motto *For Good Times And Doing Some Good*. That philosophy really was always going to sit well alongside Eric, wasn't it?

At various places along the way we found ourselves greeted with platters of food, pizza, and/or discounted drinks. A lot of this had been arranged by then-Tax Officer (yes, another one) and early joiner of the Old Bastards: Rhys Lewis.

In later days, months and years Rhys went on to get on the wrong side of a lot of people. He did so in a variety of creative ways, I must admit, but I will also say in his defence that he really could organize things.

The week after Eric I sent an email out to the GOB members in my capacity as Secretary. In part it read:

> I just wanted to say 'thanks' to everyone who participated in last Saturday's "Eric The Half-a-Brick Annual Testimonial Pub Crawl".
>
> A lot of fun was had, as well as a lot of drinks. As usual, there were very few hassles, everyone being too busy having a good time to cause trouble. The odd little misunderstanding was well smoothed over by the travelling diplomats in the group – thank you.
>
> From a G*O*Bs perspective, it was a most successful day. We signed up 17 new members, and raised $320 in donations, which will be going to the Gallipoli Foundation for research into cancer treatment. That deserves as much thanks to all of you as your excellent company!

The 'smoothing over' I mentioned really referred to an incident that I must admit I was in the middle of.

At the end of the Crawl I arrived at the Tank in the company of two mates I'd worked with in the ATO, Wayne and Tony. None of us were remotely sober, I confess. We were probably on a par with each other, but Wayne looked very much the worse for wear.

The Security person at the door of the Tank decided that Wayne was not going to be allowed to enter. He wasn't too sure about Tony or I, but was *very* sure about our mate. I didn't take that very well.

Frankly, I was indignant because of the amount of money we (Gill's Old Bastards, who I'd helped found) had put over the bar in the year. How dare this jackass try to exclude any of us? Very soon voices were raised, and so were fists.

Things were settled by the calming intervention of PK, well known in the Tank because he ran the weekly Trivia competition there as well as investing quite a bit over the bar himself. It was an awkward few minutes for him.

Poor old PK was rather shocked. He'd never seen me angry before. I think I really was, to borrow a cliché, tired and emotional. But in hindsight, raising over $300 in Gill's name did make me feel much better.

.oOo.

33 2008 – A LITTLE BASTARDRY

I think this was the year I was interviewed on talk-back radio by two local shock jocks trying to criticize binge drinking. (They invited me, quite out of the blue. The first contact definitely didn't come from me.) I didn't play.

All grown adults, making their own responsible decisions, I explained. No-one is forced, or coerced, into joining us. Nor into drinking to excess along the way. In fact, we look after each other. One dubious arrest in 29 years. That's a better record than the footballers you guys tout as heroes, not to mention the politicians.

That drew some huffing, puffing and waffling. An attempted lame joke or two from the interviewers but by now I wasn't letting them off the hook. We're about commemorating history and having fun while doing so, not imposing our views or values on anyone. You really should try it before being critical.

I was probably not the booze-addled idiot they were apparently expecting. The interview was cut short.

The 2008 Crawl took place on October 26. I reckon this was the year we moved to October as a 'standard', to fit between the football and cricket seasons, and miss the great Bathurst race for Sharon's sake (having failed to do so once and not been allowed to forget subsequently).

By now Eric was himself a card-carrying Old Bastard – number 351898, to be precise, and you can bet his card goes on Crawls with him. That'd be an expensive time to have to buy a round as per Rule 5!
(Membership card or badge must be carried at all times. Failure to produce same when challenged by fellow O.B. incurs a penalty of one round of drinks.)

He was carried on a royal blue satin pillow, secured by a gold rope (actually a curtain pull, if I remember right) as a 'seat belt'.

Since the Byron Bluesfest at Easter I had been, as Facebook so delicately puts it, "In A Relationship". It only lasted a little over a year before we realised we weren't quite right for each other, but as was observed by others, it did get me smiling again. One of the things that Julie and I shared was the entirety of the 2008 Crawl.

The other starters, although many wore the teal polo shirts, were almost divisible into two categories: Eric's past companions, and the new Old Bastards. In later years that distinction has blurred beyond recognition, I'm delighted to say.

The 'experienced hands' joining Julie and I were Lurch, Jill, Robbo, Shaz, Sandra and her daughter Nicci, Gregor, Rosco, Ian Mc, Marc, Paul K, Matt W., and Alastair. Lurch's daughter Sophie, and Alastair's eldest son Iain represented the Next Generation. Another debutant was my gorgeous goddaughter Sara.

Proudly representing the Old Bastards were the Wiltshire brothers Chris and Stu, Colleen, Gav, Dallas, John Tavendale, Mark Hawken and his lovely happy partner Leira.

There may be some who think it's a bit *inappropriate* for a godfather to delight in the presence of a goddaughter on a pub crawl. I refer those people to my comments to the shock jocks mentioned above. I'm very proud of Eric's annual excursion: its history and its camaraderie. The traditional role of a godfather is to help instill positive values in a new generation, and frankly I'm pretty bloody pleased that Sara 'gets' the value of friends and sharing time with them. An appreciation of some of the history of the city she calls home is no bad thing either, I reckon.

David and Val sent their apologies. They were off racking up more frequent flyer miles somewhere in the world. Geoff didn't appear either. The family was there in spirit of course, with Danielle raising a glass or three in Eric's name over in Blighty.

Despite the time of year, the weather must have been brisk – in one shot I'm in my gold leather jacket, Julie is wearing a tapestry coat, Paul K has two layers of shirts, and Gregor has on his big furry Russian hat. That admittedly was at least in part to team with his full uniform.

We returned to the Red Brick, or was it Burke's, or was it Burke's Red Brick? Whatever the name that year, it was a good start. We tipped a winning racehorse to get the day off to a great beginning. 'We' being me, Shaz and Colleen, I think. It had a terrifically coincidental name to make it an 'omen bet' – wish I could remember what it was.

Can't swear to the route, but from the Red Brick I know we included Era, the Fox, crossed the Victoria Bridge to the Criterion, and down to the Beach House, and Friday's. I've a very vague memory of including the Marriot at the bottom of Eagle St, but I could be completely wrong there.

Later arrivals on the Crawl included Sara's beau Ben (when he finally got off work), Matt T., Adam, Bushell, Ruth, and Robbo's then-new African bride. (She's now a part of history we don't talk about.)

Along the way several of the Old Bastards got into a bit of 'pranking'. Dallas recalls at the Fox a bunch of them had thrown a pile of change into the middle of the table, ready to be thrown into the Collection Tin. As big Dallas tossed his money in he looked over to Stu at the bar and said, "When he comes back I'm gonna slap him on the arse and say 'Nice one, big boy!'" Stu came back from the bar, saw everyone putting into the pile, so immediately tossed his change in.

"I'm in," he said. "What's it for?"

"You'll find out in a minute," replied Dall in his most ominous voice.

Let's just say it's a good thing that the money was all going to charity, thus softening the, er, blow.

There's a shot of Rosco and Bushell sitting together at the Beach House looking thoroughly grumpy about something. Possibly some unkind person had pointed out that they were the oldest Old Bastards in attendance. Not that there's anything wrong with that!

The Beach House is on the first floor of the Myer Centre, overlooking the intersection of Elizabeth and Edward Streets. With big open views on the two sides overlooking the streets, it's an attractive bar. I confess though, I have no idea where the 'Beach' is supposed to be. The sometime 'other' name for the place – the CBD – makes much more sense.

I can vouch for a finish at the riverside version of the Pig & Whistle, with a memory of Ruth being very emotional about something, into the accommodating ear of a very patient Alastair. I have an idea there was some sort of function on at the Tank that prevented us finishing there. I honestly don't think it was resentment at the previous year's tensions, from either side.

Shortly after the event I emailed a "Report" to Dani:
> Anyway, we had a good time, didn't get rained on too much, had zero unpleasant incidents, raised over $160 for charity as we ambled along - all good. A glass or three of Bombay Sapphire were consumed in your honour.

Another satisfying day, obviously, and I know I enjoyed the company!

.oOo.

34 ALASTAIR'S STORY

To honour Eric's 30th anniversary Alastair Wallace, no mean writer himself, composed an essay that wrapped his Pub Crawl memories and musings around the journey he took with his son to the 2008 event.

For the first time anywhere, here it is in its entirety.

THE CRAWL

Five minutes. Good. Plenty of time and it will be an easy wait. He likes this time of year. Winter, such as it is in Brisbane, is behind them and the stifling, energy sapping humidity of summer is yet to arrive. Still, always best to be early for Brisbane's buses. He doesn't want to be late, not today. He has the whole day in front of him and he intends to make full use of all of it for today is the day of the Crawl.

The Eric the Half-a-Brick Annual Memorial Pub Crawl is an institution. Not a well known one, granted, but an institution nonetheless. Nor is it a quintessentially Brisbane one. A quick Google of "pub crawl" will bring you hundreds of results even if you restrict the search to Australian pages. To his mind, its great distinction lies in its longevity. He's not aware that any records are kept on such matters but at 30 years old he fondly imagines it to be one of the longest continuous crawls. Every year since 1979 the Crawl has been staged. There's another thing he thinks sets it apart: its founder and chief organizer has attended every Crawl. Despite living at various times in Canberra, Adelaide and Beechworth, he has always made it back to Brisbane for his beloved Crawl; he has always been there to honour Eric whom he rescued from devastation.

The bus arrives, coming down the slope of Waterworks Road. He climbs aboard but this year, for the first time, he's not alone. This year, a new generation is joining the Crawl. His eldest son has turned 18 and is along for the ride. That will make two newbies. The daughter of another old stager has been along before but she too has now turned 18 so it will be her first 'official' outing.

The Crawl does have a distinctly Brisbane feature, one which lies at the core of its existence; is, in fact, its raison d'être. The Crawl commemorates a dark day in Brisbane's history or, more correctly, a dark night, a night that has gone down in infamy. That night was the twenty-first of April 1979. It was the night that the Belle Vue Hotel was destroyed. And Eric himself...? Eric is a half a brick which went sailing over the protective fences surrounding the demolition site as the crowds watched helpless; impotently witnessing the demise of a grand old lady. Having escaped the carnage, Eric was rescued and given a new home and the honour due to him. Every year that honour is renewed as he's carried through the pubs of Brisbane on his own velvet cushion. At each pub he's given a libation – which makes for a very soggy cushion at the end of the day.

The bus rolls past the schools his children attended in quick succession – first The Gap State School then The Gap High School. His son is in a gap year, having had enough of studying for a while. From there it's on over the old Walton Bridge. The new one, built for the widening of Waterworks Road to two lines either way all the way into the Normanby, carries traffic in the other direction.

His son asks how long he's been attending the Crawl but he's not sure – no-one is. There was an attempt made a few years ago to work it out but no-one could agree on a start date and the official record contains no reference to his presence on that first Crawl. He'll make sure that that omission does not occur with his son. He knows it was the year that the Crawl started at the Grand Chancellor up on Leichardt Street in Spring Hill. One of the crawlers brought his young daughter along – yes, the one who's officially joining the Crawl this year – so at the earliest it was 1990. Mid '93 he moved to Lismore, which meant a forced hiatus of three years before he returned to Brisbane. So the latest the start could have been was '92. He thinks he went on three Crawls before moving so he's set the date at 1990. He's happy with that and if anyone wants to object, well... that's their prerogative. It doesn't worry him.

He watches a golfer tee off at Ashgrove Golf Course. It looks a short hole from the road, possibly par 3 but that's only a guess. The golfer's swing looks cramped, awkward, the head of the club coming down too close to his feet. Then again, who's he to say? The little golf he watches is restricted to Tiger Woods on news bulletins. Compared to him – the epitome of fluid motion – anyone would look awkward.

The Crawl is not just about booze. One regular is a teetotaller. Nor is it about downing as much as possible in as quick a time as possible. Quality is prized over quantity and those charged with planning the route look for variety in a pub's offerings. It can mean some expensive stops but all the more reason to savour the drop on offer. Brisbane has grown up a lot since that first Crawl – even since his own first one. No longer is the same beer served up at every pub. Now there's beer from all over the world. As the Crawl winds its way through the city's fringes he can sample some of Australia's finest brews; in the city itself, Ireland is well represented and the rest of the British Isles feature significantly. Belgium is now securely on the map and the rest of continental Europe rates an honourable mention. So yes, booze is an integral part of the Crawl – as it should be on any self-respecting pub crawl. But there are Crawlers he sees only once a year so it's a time to catch up, to swap stories. How're the children? Good, Jeannie started pre-school this year. How's yours? That's my eldest over there talking to Marcus. Really! I remember him as a babe in arms. Sure doesn't seem all that long ago.

The St. John's Wood turnoff is approaching. The bus moves to the inside lane for the climb up the hill to West Ashgrove, the bus driver positioning herself for the turn into Coopers Camp Road. He has been chatting with his son but his eye is drawn to the creek bank here where creek and road run almost side by side. When he moved to The Gap following the return from Lismore, that bank was overgrown with weeds and straggly grasses. S.O.W.N. got stuck in and cleared out all the exotic plants. The few natives they found – stunted, neglected, struggling against the invaders – they nurtured and protected. They brought in mulch; they mobilized local residents; they transformed the bank. Now it's alive with native wildlife that's found a haven where they can feed and breed. S.O.W.N. seeded the creek with fingerlings. Now it too has re-found its former life.

It's not just on this isolated section that change has been wrought. All along this stretch of the creek – down past the reserve and the bike path – S.O.W.N. has been active. He regularly runs there and knows the joy of seeing the plants prosper and grow. It's a pleasure running there, running *in the clean air where the trees have stripped it of pollution and replaced toxins with life giving oxygen.*

The Crawl has another purpose beyond drinking. It's not a fundraiser as such but a fundraiser it has become. Its sole justification remains remembrance of the Bellevue; its sole rule is enjoyment. A tin can has joined Eric himself as an integral accoutrement to the Crawl. At each pub someone rattles the tin and collects donations for another venerable institution, the Australasian Order of Old Bastards. Patrons give what they can and no-one asks for more. Pub patrons are a generous lot in Brisbane but Crawlers have found that the more upmarket the pub the less the donations. Maybe the patrons of these establishments are too used to getting something for their 'donation' – sporting memorabilia in an auction or some such.

The bus has reached the far end of Coopers Camp Road. He counts the cars in the queue waiting to turn into Jubilee Terrace. Even on the weekend, this is a cow of an intersection. Thank God – or the Lord Mayor – that this Bus Only lane was retained. Otherwise they'd still be here ten minutes later.

As they turn he looks towards Wilston, over the ridges and the valleys where creeks once ran. It's a leafy vista as far as the eye can see. It looks spacious with plenty of room for everyone. He knows looks can be deceptive. In the older suburbs the worker's cottages are disappearing, replaced by flats and town houses. Some still survive – lovingly restored by their owners – but they're becoming a minority. People are being crammed in here where the infrastructure is already in place. Vacant blocks are being sold so small that the house fills it with no room for children to play outdoors. It means lower development costs and more blocks on the available land so profits are higher.

Still, from this vantage, it looks verdant and he concentrates on that. He doesn't want to dwell on negative thoughts, doesn't want anything to cast a shadow on this day.

Yet a shadow does cross his line of sight. He looks up. A cloud is scuttling along, pushed by a light breeze. Most years, they've been lucky with the weather but he remembers one year where it poured relentlessly. It was before he moved to Lismore. He tries to pin a year to it but can't. All he can remember is that it was the day before the big Drought Relief auction held above the Indian restaurant in Southbank. It poured that day too. How ironic it seemed at the time that a drought relief auction was being held on a day of pouring rains. He supposed Dorothea McKellar would have appreciated it.

He bought a preserving kit for friends on a farm outside Armidale. He wonders if they still have it. The only time he'd seen it used was to boil Bruce the Goose for an Australia Day dinner. It turned out the goose was actually a gander but the name was too good to throw out on a mere technicality.

The bus slows as it approaches the roundabout where LaTrobe joins McGregor Terrace for the run up the hill to Bardon shops. When he's been coming up Given Terrace, he's been thankful for buses coming in the other direction. They interrupt the flow of traffic down past the Governor's backyard and give him an opportunity to turn. In peak hour, such opportunities can be few and far between.

A question from his son, one his partner raised earlier, brings to mind a very important point about the Crawl. There hasn't been a single unsavoury incident on the Crawl in all its thirty years – no brawls, no sexual assaults, no drunken idiots exposing themselves. They leave such rank stupidity to footballers. The closest they've come to trouble was some policemen trying to stop the inaugural crawl but passers-by stepped in and convinced the cops they weren't harming anyone.

There was an award at one stage – the 'Frozen Broccoli Award' – for the person who injured himself or herself in the most spectacular fashion. Its origins are lost in the mists of conjecture and reminiscence but all agree that it got its name from the use of a packet of frozen broccoli to tend an injured leg. The packet was pressed into use for want of the more traditional icepack. The award has slipped into neglect in recent years. Perhaps, he reflects, with age has come wisdom and a tempering of the foolhardiness which leads to taking unwarranted risks. Then again, perhaps they're just drinking less.

They're on Given Terrace now, well past the halfway point on the journey. On the left there's a lingerie shop. He takes it as another indication of how much this city has grown up. When he moved to Brisbane, more than twenty years ago now, such a shop would not have existed – not here in clear view in the middle of suburbia. Who knows what sort of perverts and deviates it would have attracted? Not only that, it would have corrupted the innocent schoolboys travelling past on their way to the local Marist college. The college is gone now – another sad demise – but plenty of schoolchildren still travel past every day on the bus on their way to State High or one of the many private schools dotted around the fringes of the city.

The shop presents an extensive display of good quality lingerie with no hint at pretence. He casts a surreptitious glance in the shop window's direction but the bus quickly passes and the view is gone, replaced as they round a couple of bends by the antiques shops around the old Paddington cinema.

The mode of transport between pubs is walking. It gives the opportunity for groups to break up and reform and provides some worthwhile exercise. They like to think the exercise works off some of the alcohol and no amount of scientific evidence to the contrary is going to dissuade them of this belief. There is however, as there should be for every good rule, an exception. Brisbane is the River City so it's beholden on Crawl organizers to include at least one ferry trip. Anyway, the Story Bridge Hotel is on the other side of the river and it beckons like a siren. Its problem is that it's isolated from other pubs. One year, the Crawlers walked from the Valley but it was not a successful experiment. By the time the stragglers arrived – complaining that the walk resulted in far too long a time between drinks – the faster walkers had already finished their drink. Impatient to be off to the next pub and fully aware that that involved a river crossing – and, quite possibly, a wait for the next ferry – the quick ones readily agreed with this analysis. The Crawl has not crossed the bridge since.

They don't stop at Paddington. That surprises him and he comments on this to his son. He's used to this route in peak hour – the bus always stops then. Paddington Central is as busy as usual but now it's shoppers, not commuters filling its footpaths. He notes that the eateries are doing a brisk trade – not surprising on such a fine morning. He can imagine the routine: walk up to the shops, or drive if you live further away, do your shopping then a relaxing cup of tea or coffee with maybe a nice snack to go with it.

The ferry trip is the time for singing. 'Gilligan's Island' is the song of choice and has been for as long as he can remember. He considers it an eminently suitable ditty for a brief trip on the water. Occasionally, murmurs are heard that singing this particular song could invite bad karma but such negative vibes are quickly and firmly suppressed. He's been trying to teach the words to his son and hopes he'll remember enough to muddle through. Not that it'll probably matter; what the singing lacks in ability it more than makes up for with enthusiasm. It's just that his son has a good voice and he could acquit himself well if he gets the words right.

It's a sign of the age of most of the crawlers that another popular ditty is 'F Troop'. Ah, they don't write TV themes like that anymore. It's good though that a new generation is joining the Crawl. It needs new blood, needs people to carry the flame as the old stagers inevitably fade away. It would be sad to see the Crawl become nothing more than a memory; something which, like the hotel which gave rise to it, becomes the stuff of legend; stories that old people tell to incredulous grandchildren who know nothing of what it was like to be part of the Crawl in its heyday.

Ithaca Pool is full. This time of day it's all families at play. The exercisers doing their laps have long since vacated their lanes and the Latin Aqua Aerobics and other classes are all mid-week. Now it's all laughing, splashing children.

Lang Park is on the right. It's known by some sponsor's name now but to him it will always be Lang Park. It's quiet now. The footy season is over so the venue has withdrawn into its summer hibernation. He expresses the opinion to his son that for more than half the year it's a white elephant, sucking up funds to maintain it for no useful purpose beyond sitting there empty, waiting for the crowds to roll up again come the new season next year. At least the Gabba has cricket in the summer, he says. This place has nothing.

Singing is not confined to the ferry ride. Karaoke bars get a work out from those interested in such things. He isn't one of them. Fortunately, he reflects, his son didn't inherit that particular gene. Unfortunately, by the latter stages of the Crawl, interest often exceeds capability. It's one thing for enthusiasm to exceed ability when you're part of a group; it's another thing completely when you're by yourself. One Crawler even went so far as to try to explain away silent passages in his rendition of a popular tune as singing the harmony line but pitching it beyond the range of human hearing. As evidence, he cited the barking of local dogs. No-one had the heart to suggest that barking in accompaniment was actually howling in complaint.

Then too, there was the year they got off the ferry at the pier at the bottom of Eagle Street. A bridal party was hovering nearby. Maybe they'd emerged from a reception in the nearby Heritage Hotel; maybe they were waiting their turn to go in. Spontaneously, the Crawl broke into a rendition of the old Skyhooks song, 'All My Friends Are Getting Married'. It brought a smile to the face of bride and groom alike and applause from the guests as the Crawlers moved on to their next watering hole.

If there are good aspects to a city growing up there are also bad. They cross the bridge over Hale Street, a street widened to cater to the ever increasing traffic flow. When the street was widened, the old Boot Factory fell. It was expendable, it had to go because the car reigns supreme. The car must be allowed to move freely, it must be allowed to go where it will. Without the car the city will grind to a halt; with the car, the city is in dire risk of grinding to a halt.

Many are the pubs that the Crawl visited in its early years that no longer exist. Land values in the city are too great, there's more profit in renting office space than in pubs. The Lands Office, the Belfast, the Majestic, they're all gone. The Railway too, with its beautiful stained glass windows picturing peacocks. The Grosvenor is still there but it's not the same. In its courtyard was the first well sunk in Brisbane. Now its been covered over by the kitchen of a McDonalds fast food outlet – another piece of history lost forever. The Carlton and York still exist in a sense. They form part of the façade of the Myer Centre but that's all they are – façade.

At the top of Caxton Street there's similar desecration taking place. The Police barracks precinct is being refurbished. A cinema is being built which has been likened to a tipped over soft drink can. Yet another apartment block is going up, pushed so close to the back of the barracks that they can no longer be seen from Roma Street. The barracks itself remains. The graffiti has been cleaned off and new windows set into freshly painted frames. But like the York and the Carlton it's just façade, a shell. Inside it's to be more office space. That's the price being paid, the rent from the offices will repay the cost of restoration. At least, he reflects, it's better than the Treasury Building. All the beautiful pressed metal ceilings were torn out and the interior walls knocked down to make way for that palace of false hope and broken dreams called a casino. None of it is desecration on the scale of the Bellevue but it's desecration nonetheless.

He's in need of pleasant thoughts and, as if on cue, one springs to mind. For some people, merely being on the Crawl is not enough. To them, it's an opportunity to step out of their normal workaday persona and do something completely different.

One such is the resident Crawl interviewer. For the first few years it was This Is Your Life. He 'acquired' a menu from a Chinese restaurant and, with this in hand he presented their life history to unsuspecting Crawlers. He has now moved on. He dresses in shirt and tie and, armed with a clipboard and a microphone, he interviews people. Always there's a theme for the day At the time of the Napisan ads he posed as that obnoxious man who'd bale up innocent housewives and berate them about how their washing can't possibly be totally clean unless they used Napisan. He'd thrust a box of Napisan under the nose of anyone and everyone and asked what they thought of this marvelous product. No-one was safe, everyone was fair game – fellow Crawlers, pub patrons, even people sitting in their car waiting for the lights to change.

Bright young things are out and about, making their leisurely way to the pubs and restaurants at the top of Caxton Street. These pubs are on the itinerary but not this early. The Paddo – back along Caxton Street – has once again been deemed to be outside the viable range of the Crawl. After walking down from the Normanby, the L.A. and Caxton offer better prospects. Either way you look at it, Normanby to Paddo or Paddo to Transcontinental is a bit of a hike. So, once again, the Paddo misses out.

One year, an enterprising Crawler – a fresh faced youngster new to the Crawl, if he remembers rightly – suggested they go Normanby – L.A – Paddo – Caxton – Transcontinental. Such a proposal was dismissed as being far too logical for a Crawl.

There's always some point on the Crawl where splitters decide they know better than the organizers and go to a pub not on the route. He has been, he must admit, one of them. The New International on Boundary Street in Spring Hill offers a fine range of its own brews and he's been known to linger there while the body of the Crawl moves on, ostensibly to partake in lunch but actually to work his way through the beer menu. There are individual pubs in the city which are personal favourites and get the same attention and woe behold any organizer who doesn't include the Aurora for a taste of its excellent barleywine. Similarly, entertainment being provided in a pub might induce some to loiter awhile and catch up with the other Crawlers later. If it's known that a not so fancy pub is next up on the itinerary, that only increases the temptation.

The bus has turned off Roma Street onto the ramp up to the new Roma Street bus station. From there it will drop down into the tunnel under King George Square and on to the Cultural Centre. The Red Brick on Annerley Road is the starting point for this year's Crawl so a quick change at the Cultural Centre is in order for the short journey to Mater Hill. But that's the stuff of another story. Like the Crawl itself, that story extends into the future, something to be enjoyed in its own time.

The Crawl has survived for 30 years and shows no signs of declining just yet, for all his concerns. He's satisfied it's in safe hands and that there will still be Crawlers making this or a similar journey in years to come. Certainly, the Crawl has not seen the last of him – not by a long shot.

.o0o.

35 2009 – THIRTY, NOT THIRSTY

On June 10 the Premier Anna Bligh released the official list of 150 'State Icons', across 10 categories, as voted by Queenslanders over the previous months.

Ms Bligh said almost 30,000 votes were received to compile the official list, from a short-list of 300.

Category 7 was *Defining Moments*, and there at number 11 was "**Belle Vue Hotel demolished**". I was a little surprised, perhaps afraid that too many people would have forgotten that act of infamy, but delighted that Eric's birthplace had won some recognition.

The Crawl itself was set for exactly four months after Ms Bligh's announcement: 10/10/09.

In honour of the anniversary – the passing of another decade – the commemorative t-shirts returned. Printed in warning-sign yellow on black: That's THIRTY – Not *THIRSTY!* In addition to this emphatic statement were the regular Eric portrait, the GOBs logo and motto, and the Latin phrase CAPIAMUS CEREVISIUM! Helpfully I included a translation for those who don't read Classical languages: Let's grab a beer!

Again my memory is, to say the least, scratchy. I think we went back to the Valley for a change of starting venue, possibly the Royal George. I know that was a popular choice for a few Crawlers who liked to load up on a hearty breakfast early – there were a few good options nearby. Equally uncertainly, I'm presuming we were back at the Tank to finish.

Photos of the event show a range of unusual hats, although I don't remember it as a declared 'theme'. I'm in an orange-and-yellow tropical print pork pie hat, which I know I've worn a few times. It was a present from Nicci Craig. Lurch sports what looks like a genuine silk Mandarin brimless cap, while Gav looks like a Caucasian Arab, his white cloth headpiece held in place by a nice gold band.

In what I think was his only Pub Crawl appearance, Steave Beaston matched his black-and-gold t-shirt with a black pork pie hat and an elegant gold tie. Mark Hawken sported a black topper, while his partner Leira wore a floppy black 'hippy hat'. Dallas had somewhere acquired a copy of Mick Dundee's Stetson, complete with faux crocodile teeth. At least, I don't *think* they were real.

Somebody had brought a garish zombie mask. I'm not sure who, as it turns up in photos wrapped around the various faces of Mark Hawken, Dallas, and Chris Wiltshire (as well as other unidentifiables!). It looked surprisingly good with Chris' dapper grey bowler hat. The weirdest picture of the mask though was the one where Dallas somehow had managed to wear it upside down under his Crocodile Dundee hat. The Facebook post described it as "The Attack of the Upside Down Face Demon!"...

Matt Taylor wore one of the standout hats: a tall 'witches hat' striped in red, pink, orange and white, and topped with a natty pink pompom.

Dallas has a photo of me with Colleen, apparently singing "She's A Rasta Cowgirl" (to the tune of *Rhinestone Cowboy* I assume) in honour of the Bob Marley-style oversized knitted beanie she was wearing.

Among the photos is a *very* rare shot of Kat, who is *not* wearing a hat. Miss Kat was a very effective and enthusiastic Treasurer for Gill's Old Bastards, but notoriously camera-shy. Discovering that she'd been photographed, and the photo had made it onto Facebook displeased her considerably - something for which she promised Miss Coll was going to get into serious trouble when they both got back to work.

Like I said, my memory of this year's Crawl is sadly lacking, especially given that it was a Significant Anniversary. I dunno – maybe all those hats went to my head?

One thing I do know is that I'd had the bright idea (?) to walk home to

Tarragindi at the end of the Crawl. Possibly I'd figured it would be good for my health.

Certainly the athletes in our group (Alastair, for instance) would probably endorse a long walk as a healthful activity. Perhaps less so with a skinful of gin with subtle overtones of beer.

Wobbly but determined, I'd made it all the way to the edge of Fairfield by somewhere around midnight. Just the time to be staggering past the cemetery.

As I stepped unsteadily out to cross the street, a taxi came belting up the hill at a speed well over the limit. Well, I was over the limit, so perhaps that was only fair. He didn't see me in time to brake, I was in no condition to dodge.

My old Dad used to say, "God favours fools and drunks." Certainly true on this occasion - I bounced off the cab. The cab that stopped for a few seconds, but had sped off by the time I'd hauled myself upright.

Somehow, remarkably, there were no obvious broken bones. (See Dad's comment above.) There was some skin missing where I'd hit the road, and what turned into large and colourful bruises on my ribs, leg and back. I was definitely too bloody sore to walk the rest of the way home.

Eventually another cab (different driver, presumably different vehicle - I didn't see an obvious me-shaped dent) came along and I made my uncomfortable way home.

It would have been nice to have been able to call for a cab instead of the long forlorn wait at the side of the road, but my mobile phone's battery was flat.

I was just glad that I wasn't.

.o0o.

36 2010 – SORRY, I MISSED THAT...

Well, I didn't actually *miss* it. Certainly I was there. I just remember very, very little of the actual event.

I'd had a big start to the year. A numerically significant birthday. A Tax Sports Carnival in Perth, complete with a long-sought gold medal in bowls. Six or seven weeks overseas in the UK and Morocco. Meeting a wonderful lady on-line. Marrying her. Yep, I'd been busy.

Reckon I'll use that as an excuse for remembering so little of Eric's annual Big Day.

I can tell you that it was the first experience of a Crawl for my darling bride Meredith. She does still reckon she enjoyed it, and has made as many subsequent appearances as our sometimes hectic lifestyle allows.

Late in the day, we think, someone stole the charity collection tin. A very low act, and we can only hope karma is all it's cracked up to be. If the person who nicked it truly desperately needed the money, well, alright – it was always intended to "do some good".

If on the other hand it was just some lazy, greedy, dishonest villain, then in a perfect world they will have cut themselves on the tin when trying to get it open, the wound will have gotten infected from some germ off a bar or table where the tin had been sitting, and the perpetrator will have had to get their thieving hand amputated. Sometimes I like to let my imagination off its leash.

This was the year that a small number of us went from the Crawl (specifically, the Pig & Whistle at the riverside) to Pretty Boy's 60th birthday party at Café Verde in Chermside. Pretty Boy was yet another Tax Officer in our social circle: an old drinking buddy and card-carrying Old Bastard. I'm really not sure how he'd never got to make it onto an Eric Crawl. Perhaps his beloved Kath somehow managed to keep him safe.

Café Verde was the bar in the Chermside Green Motel, and the regular lunchtime haunt of past Crawlers such as Tony Anstis, Wayne O'Keefe, Rhys Lewis, and Terry McFarland. And yours truly when I occupied a desk in the Chermside Branch of the ATO. It was demolished a little while ago to make room for yet more car parking for the shopping centre there – an edifice that's growing like The Blob in the old horror movie.

Rosco was one of those on the birthday party guest list, and was fretting about being late because I was (typically) taking my time over farewells to various Crawlers.

Presumably others went up the road to the Tank, but without Eric (who I'm pretty sure I didn't relinquish) would that count as part of the Crawl? It can't be an Eric without Eric, surely...

Meredith drove, which clearly indicates that she either spent the Crawl not drinking (highly unlikely) or more probably saw us off at the start, then rejoined us at or near the finish line in time to leave.

She describes me as having been very hammered, but in a cheerful sort of way. As part of Pretty Boy's celebration there was karaoke happening at Verde. I apparently did a surprisingly respectable job of *Devil Went Down To Georgia*, using the original lyrics even – not Gilligan's Island.

The description of 'cheerful' is no surprise. Overzealous Security staff excepted there have been very few times over the years when I haven't been happy on our annual celebration of Eric.

.o0o.

37 2011 – CALLING 'TIME' ON THE TANK

Another blank page in my memory. For what I do have here I'm indebted to Adam Cretier's photos from a Facebook album called Eric Crawls Again.

Those photos give the date of the Crawl as 16 October, so we'd clearly become settled on the 'between the sports seasons' concept.

One cheerful shot shows Renoir, Cathy Moss, Leigh Horsfall, Matt Taylor, Brett and Gregor in a bar festooned with red balloons, and surrounded by young ladies in very German outfits. Maybe the Melbourne Hotel. Though it looks right for Oktoberfest, I don't think it's the German Club. I'm sure it would be another six years before we'd actually get around to putting that establishment on a Crawl.

Another photograph shows me and Lurch with his daughter Sophie, looking very much more grown up than on her first few Eric photos.

There's also a curious shot of Cathy standing, well, sort of, with one foot up in the air. It could have been 1.) a new dance, 2.) a Monty Python Ministry of Silly Walks re-enactment, or 3.) the only way to get decent reception on her mobile phone.

One of the 'survivors' at the Tank was Leigh, who described herself on Facebook as "looking FAB after twentyish G & Ts. Now you know why I was in dire need of a fry-up!"

Ah yes, the fry-up. A time honoured post-Crawl breakfast. Or even dinner for the intestinally hardy. I'm not sure which meal Leigh was referring to in this case.

I'm not a big eater on Pub Crawls, although I'm told it would be better for me if I was. Something about food absorbing alcohol. But food has been an important part of the event for many people for years.

From real food, like the excellent Italian at Topolino's and Lucky's, to the other end of the spectrum: over-processed 'fast food' at any of the infamous chains of "family restaurants" where nutrition runs a long second to convenience.

I do concede the importance of a good pre-Eric breakfast though. I know that for some long-standing Crawlers there was actually quite a tradition of getting together for said meal. Unfortunately, some of the best venues for that gathering in both the City and the Valley have also gone the way of so many of the pubs.

We didn't know it at the time, but it was to be the Tank's last appearance on a Pub Crawl. The pub's closure a few months later was very sudden, catching us so off-guard that a few pieces of Gill's Old Bastards memorabilia, like our Certificate of Charter, vanished into the swirling black hole of The Administrators. No value to anyone but the GOBs, I've never quite understood why we were never able to get them back. Phone calls and messages went unreturned.

I'm very glad we resisted the occasional thought of having a 'display case' and making the place a permanent home for Eric!

.o0o.

38 2012 – 33 AND 1/2, SOME KIND OF A RECORD

It might have been nice to set a date in August, just to have some fun with the $33^{1/3}$ anniversary of the Belle Vue's destruction.

(For the benefit of young people reading this, many years ago, long playing records, or LPs, rotated on turntables at $33^{1/3}$ revolutions per minute, or RPM. This was how we listened to music before Spotify, MP3, Compact Discs or even cassettes. Eh? What's a 'cassette'? Oh... I give up...)

By now though, the October date had become well established, and the 27th of the month was promoted well in advance.

The route was planned by Gregor, whose fondness for, and residency in, the south side of town was reflected in his choices.

Gabba	Chalk	Brewhouse
Ship Inn	CBD	Archive 1
Lock'n'Load	Music Café	Boundary
Archive 2	Era	Terminus
The Joynt	Queenslander	Transcontinental
Tin Billy	Grosvenor	Criterion

I'm really struck by how much West End has changed over the life of the Crawl. In my University days a lot of the suburb was at the bottom end of working class. There was a big migrant population, a lot of unemployment, and not much money. The pubs reflected that – there was nothing flash about the Boundary in those days, and while the Melbourne was trying to be 'up-market' not a lot of us were convinced.

Fast forward to 2012 and beyond and the landscape is very different. Many of the buildings are still there, although some of the interiors have been radically 'made over'. The average age of the local population has gone down, and the average income has gone up. Now the streets of West End are well supplied with boutique bars selling a lot more than the standard local domestic beers.

They sell some of them at high prices, too, and that fact caused a bit of disquiet among Crawlers counting their pennies across twenty-one pubs.

Only slightly further afield from West End, The Gabba was certainly not the classic old pub it used to be. The name had been attached to what was just a rather soul-less ground floor room in a glass-and-chrome office and apartment block. The service was polite but hardly enthusiastic.

The starters were Colleen, Shaz, Gregor, Renoir, Lurch, Ian McLeod, Iain Moore, PK, Gav, Josh Blinco and Matt Richards.

I'm sure the numbers swelled across the day, but I'll be honest and admit that, again, my memory fails me.

Taking a leaf from the Downunder Bar's book, the Tin Billy on George Street caters primarily for backpackers. In recent years there's been a proliferation of hostels appear from the end of George Street up along Roma Street and the Petrie Terrace area. It makes sense that there'd be a watering hole dedicated to that market, although us locals were made welcome too.

Further along George, the old Grosvenor's latest identity was as a topless bar. Well, the bar had a top, but the young ladies working behind it didn't wear any. Tops. Lurch was with Sophie – old enough to drink legally but still young enough to be Impressionable he thought. So they gave the dubious delights of the Grosvenor a miss, went straight on to the Criterion, and shared a jug of Cosmopolitan (cocktail by the jug?!?) until we all caught up.

The Tank had suddenly closed mid-year. There followed several weeks of 'trial runs', experimental visits and negotiations with various pubs. In September the Cri became the new 'home' of Gill's Old

Bastards. With that honour came the prestige of being the final stop on Eric's annual testimonial.

I'm not sure that the staff always see the arrival of a squad of Pub Crawl 'survivors' as a prestigious thing, but we mean well.

.o0o.

39 2013 – BON VOYAGE

When Gill and I had moved back to Brisbane in 1999, it was clear in my head at least that it was not intended to be a permanent move. We'd moved because of work.

I had long since decided that hot humid weather did not agree with me, and Brisbane has that for a big chunk of the year. Meredith hasn't got quite my enthusiasm for cold weather, but was certainly keen to find somewhere more temperate.

To suggest we had a Plan would be overstating it. We sold the house and temporarily moved into a friend's unit while he was travelling. Ah, travelling – that was the key. We'd high-tail it out of Brisbane for the USA, then the UK and Europe and then… well, we'd see.

So where did that leave the Pub Crawl?

As a bloody impressive 'Bon voyage' party, that's where. We held a slightly more formal gathering at the German Club the week before, but it was on July 6th that we got together with the Close Personal Friends of Eric for last drinks before departure.

The advertised route was as follows:

Royal George	Wickham	Elephant & Wheelbarrow
Marriott	Orient *(if they surprise us by being open)*
Pig & Whistle	Fridays	Stamford
Port Office	Belgian	Victory
Stock Exchange	Embassy	

then the run up the Queen St. Mall
finishing at the Criterion

Given the excitement of our impending travels, I think I can be excused for not remembering much of the day. I'm sure, though, that I appreciated the cooler weather

As in previous years, there was a market happening in the Brunswick Street Mall, and I think its siren call was too much for Meredith to resist a bit of last-minute pre-holiday shopping. I can't complain, having succumbed to the same temptaion to shop on previous Crawls.

This may have been the Crawl where Anne won the Frozen Broccoli early with a fall outside one of the Valley bars. Her ankle blew up pretty much immediately. The manager of the bar was supremely uninterested in offering any assistance at all, *until* Wayne mentioned how many lawyers we collectively knew and worked with.

Only then did a taxi appear right at the door, with remarkable alacrity, to get Anne and Wayne safely home. Funny that.

Speaking of taxis, I'm reminded of an old story of Rocky, the Sri Lankan bongo drummer and 'prominent West End identity'. Poignant to remember, as I think it was about this year that Rocky passed away, succumbing to years of overuse of a number of substances, of which alcohol was amongst the more benign.

But the taxi story: it was the journey home at the end of a Crawl, and not unusually, Rocky knew of a party to which everyone sharing the cab with him was of course invited. He blearily navigated to what he reckoned was the right street, but wasn't sure of the house. Near the end of the street he suddenly exclaimed, "No! It's back there a bit!"

The cab driver obligingly reversed the taxi back a ways... further... further...

"Nope. Nope. Up there a bit," says Rocky, pointing ahead.

Driver shrugged and drove on, back to almost the same spot as before, where his Sri Lankan navigator decided, "No, it *is* back there."

After the third or fourth journey back and fro along the same street, the cabbie, sick of this, pulled over and ordered everyone out. As the taxi speeds away, Rocky looks around, sees the house they've been deposited outside, and announces, "Yeah! This is the place!"

And remarkably, it was. Rocky was a character, and he's missed.

Back to 2013. For all that we managed our Crawling pretty carefully, and pulled up excited but otherwise well at the Cri, Meredith and I shouted ourselves a couple of nights and a Recovery Day in one of the city's nicer apartments.

Eric was fostered into the tender care of Gregor and Dougie, as I recall. Both gentlemen with a strong sense of history, so it was a household where I was confident that the remnant of the Belle Vue would be cared for and respected.

And about 36 hours after the completion of the Crawl, my darling bride and I skipped the country.

.o0o.

40 2014 – ELEVEN ON THE ELEVENTH

Meredith and I were back in Australia in late March – somewhat earlier than anticipated due to a combination of circumstances. We visited Brisbane only fleetingly on our return though. Just long enough to share a few drinks and pick up Eric, really.

A few months in Hervey Bay culminated in my being "Grand Marshall" for Maryborough's annual city-wide Pub Crawl. This was a terrific fun event that raised very good money to support research into Alzheimers Disease. I'm pleased to report that a few of Eric's nearest and dearest travelled up from Brisbane for the occasion – I know Gregor, Megan and Sharon were there.

After our spell at the Bay we moved down to the NSW Northern Rivers region, beginning what has become a whole new lifestyle for us as professional house-sitters.

Being 'out of the loop' as regards Pub Crawl planning, as the advertised date drew near I started to get a bit anxious. On September 27 I sent a worried email to Alastair, Adam & Lurch, thinking that one of them might have taken (or been given) some responsibility. It read, in part:

> Not sure if your diary is appropriately noted, but this year's Eric has long been scheduled for 11 October.
>
> Said date is starting to loom large, and I can't see any way of my getting to BrizVegas beforehand to plan any sort of a route.
>
> I considered saying "Let's start at the Royal George & finish at the Criterion and make it up as we go along in between" but that seems... well, foolhardy is probably too mild a word.

A full scale rehearsal probably would be overkill, but suggestions, observations and information as to what bars are open (esp twixt 10 and 12) - and even which ones still exist (I really don't get to Brisbane often) would be most welcome.

Thank you gentlemen - looking forward to seeing you all on 11/10!

It was Sharon who came up with a suggested itinerary three days later, and it was a good one. Good enough to be enthusiastically adopted.

The actual route was delightfully simple – pretty well only three streets to navigate. Down Edward and back up, Elizabeth and then into George. Easy walking, for those of us not as young as we were (35 years ago...).

The itinerary itself went like this:

Grand Central (*ex-Fihellys*)	Stock Exchange	Victory
Belgium Bier Café	Stamford	Port Office
Embassy	Beach House	Irish Murphys
The Villager	Criterion	

In the email that went out to Old Bastards around the country I made the observation:
> It'd be grand if you could join us. Don't let being an "out of towner" stop you - it's never stopped me and it won't stop me this year - I'd love to see as many of you as possible.

Sadly, though, I don't remember any other non-Brisbane folks travelling to join Meredith and I.

Dallas recalls a conversation early in the piece that, "after last year, we shouldn't collect any more beer mats." Apparently someone has quite a sizeable collection. Neither he nor I can imagine to whom that could *possibly* refer. Certainly neither of us, as he noted we've never carried bags big enough to put them in.

There are a couple of almost identical photos taken at the Stamford –

a 'birds eye' view from the upstairs gallery. The photographers were me and rookie Crawler James Prendergast. Visible below are the smiling faces of Meredith, Wayne, Anne, Eleanor, Matt T., Sharon, Ruth, PK, Gav, Lurch, John Tav, Iain, Funsize, Matt W, Matt Richards, Josh, Adam, Dallas, Ian McLeod, Libby, Stu Wiltshire, and a couple of faces I recognise but can't put names to. Clearly, a pretty good turnout.

Later in the day, mid-afternoon I reckon, we were upstairs in the Beach House. In one photo I can see in the middle of the table Eric on his plush red cushion, and a tall glass cylinder no longer full of beer, the tap having been serving PK, Gav, Dallas, Tav, James P. and Chris Wiltshire.

The Old Bastards clearly *get* the whole Pub Crawl thing. Hardly surprising...

.o0o.

41 2015 – PUBLICLY TRANSPORTED

Gavin Shaw took on the responsibility of planning the route this year, and came up with something new and different. No mean feat after thirty-six years!

We'd flirted with 'fringe' and suburban pubs in previous years, but Gav took it to a whole new level, starting us out at the Indooroopilly Hotel on October 17. (I'm sure it was just a coincidence that it's his local watering hole…)

The Indro welcomed us though, and its proximity to the railway station meant that quite a few starters were able to get out into the wilds of the Western Suburbs.

It's a pub that holds quite a few memories. It was Filthy Foley's regular haunt, and I shared several rounds of ales with him there before his health failed. Many years earlier the Indro's bottle shop provided much of the lubrication for *Origin* – the gone-but-not-quite-forgotten band of the 70's that featured Robbo The Non-Existent on bass, and a lead singer who went by the name of Johnny B. Scotland before becoming Renoir.

Some of us remember a movie launch at the nearby cinema decades ago that included a performance by a troupe of pretty young disco roller skaters. Among that troupe was a young Wayne Hunter, cutting moves long before the invention of ski machines.

There was a photo taken at the start, of the 'old bloke' attendees. There were Eric, Ern and Renoir from '79, Robbo from soon after, the Matthews Taylor and Walker, and Gregor. All of us proud of our 'veteran' status.

Sharon, Jolie, Libby and Gav were there as well, but none of them could fairly be called old blokes (although I must recognise that Sharon in particular has logged an impressive number of Pub Crawl miles over thirty-odd years). If PK was there at the start he didn't make it into a photo. I suspect it was a bit later in the day when he joined, possibly as early as Pub #2.

The teal polo shirts that had served Gill's Old Bastards faithfully for a few years had started to suffer with age. PK and Colleen had organised new white polos, embroidered with a small colourful 'handprint' design, and several of these were worn on the day.

In my continuing search for sartorial elegance (and just to be different) I'd bought myself a shiny blue satin shirt to wear over my white polo. I quickly became quite fond of the shirt, but never got to wear it again. I made the mistake of trying to iron it after its post-Crawl wash. What I know about that particular domestic chore could be written on the back of a postage stamp (and still leave room for a chapter of this book). The shirt melted, or dissolved or burned or something. It further reinforced my belief that the only place for an iron is on the golf course.

From the Indro we all walked up the hill to the Pig & Whistle – yes, *another* one. This version of the Pig was home to PK's Trivia longer than any of the other bars he regularly worked, and was much revered by many Old Bastards because of it.

The next move was onto the bus stop. The actual route is only vague in my mind, but I do remember some confusion around what bus we were supposed to be catching. Maybe to the City, or maybe Toowong? I have a recollection of catching the CityCat ferry from outside the Regatta, but perhaps my wires are getting crossed with an earlier Crawl.

Somehow or other we got to the south side of town. Lurch and Megan joined us there, appearing in photos taken in the Archive and the Melbourne.

There were some energetic Crawlers who walked on from there, in the rain I think, but I know I was among a number who jumped on a convenient bus.

 We must have timed our arrival at the Grand Central fortuitously – there were platters of party pies and sausage rolls being served. Gregor insisted on my wearing a napkin so as not to risk spoiling my nice new white shirt. I don't think he was as concerned about the shiny blue one. Adam joined us there I think, possibly arriving by train.

 It was in a dark bar, I think perhaps the Britannia (or whatever name it was trading under then) that I noticed that Matt W. wasn't his usually cheery self. I asked him what was wrong, and he explained that three blokes he knew or worked with had died recently. One wrapped his shiny new sports car round a tree, one was a suicide, and the other might as well have been – attacking armed policemen with a large knife and getting shot. All three had not long turned 40 or 45, an age that Matt was staring down the barrel of himself, a prospect now severely worrying him.

"It's that mid-life crisis thing, isn't it? What's the story with that?" he asked plaintively.

 I truthfully had no answer for him, but I did promise I'd try to find out anything that might reassure him. That promise became a project that became a book – *Mid-Life Crisis MANagement – A Quiet Word about Male Menopause and Surviving Middle Age.* It's done pretty well. I'm told it's helped some blokes (which was the whole idea so I'm very pleased) and it launched me on the path of writing more and podcasting about men's health. All starting with a quiet conversation on a Pub Crawl. Thanks Matt, thank Eric.

 I don't know if it was our little chat that lifted Matt's dark mood (I'd like to think it helped) but he was definitely in better spirits by the time we reached the riverside version of the Pig & Whistle. The pub has a unisex washroom connecting the male and female toilets. In one of the basins Matt found an almost full bottle of perfume, and shrewdly thought it would make a good present for his beloved and patient wife Jen.

When he got it home, he decided he'd better give it the 'sniff test' first. His first thought apparently was, "Gee, that smells like a stripper."

No, not a paint stripper, the fleshier kind.

Jen approached, noticed the aroma (faintly like coconut, apparently) and said, "That smells like a stripper."

While Matt was pleased to have his opinion supported, he apparently did quietly wonder how his good lady wife knew what a stripper smelled like.

Speaking of good ladies, there's a nice photo of PK and Jolie looking romantic at the Riverside Pig & Whistle. It was the early days of their courtship, as I recall.

And I know I was very glad to be joined by my own good lady when Meredith caught up with us in the latter part of the Crawl. Much as I enjoy opportunities to 'play the single bloke', it's also pretty special to share one of my favourite days of the year with someone I love.

Once again we finished at the Criterion. I'm quite sure that there was more than five of us there at the end, but the photo I've seen shows me and Eric with Meredith, Gregor, Sponsie (great nickname, short for Responsible Adult, coined on a winery bus trip), and a beaming Robbo.

I think Robbo's big healthy grin may have had something to do with him having quietly skipped a couple of stops in our big cross-town Crawl. Well, the rule has always been that there are no rules.

.oOo.

42 2016 – A BIT UP-MARKET

A few weeks before the 2016 event (on Saturday 8 October) the new GOBs Secretary, Barb Tate, sent out an email inviting members to Party with Eric to raise some money for Gill's Old B@st@rds' charities.

Obviously some peoples' email servers were blocking GOBs' mail. Despite our history, and the long and proud history of the phrase itself, it seems some computer systems and networks have filters that don't like the word Bastard. Sigh.

Anyway, the route got off to another south side start.

Boundary	Lock & Load	Archive
Melbourne	Pig & Whistle West End	
Saccharomyces	The Fox	Irish Murphy's
Beach House	Embassy	Victory
Stock Exchange	O'Malleys	Criterion

One for the lovers of boutique beers, for the first half anyway! A bit tough on the wallet, too. And yes, yet another Pig & Whistle...

For those of you who aren't scientifically inclined, the name 'Saccharomyces' is a Greek word that literally means 'sugar fungus'. It's usually called 'brewers yeast'.

O'Malleys was the latest name for what had been the Britannia Inn, and prior to that Her Majesty's. It was a downstairs bar that got progressively smaller as bits of the 'footprint' were sold off to make room for more shops. Sort of a basement version of what's happened to the Embassy Hotel over the years.

The old front bar of the Embo was where I used to enjoy people watching out a window overlooking the intersection of Edward and

Elizabeth Streets over lunch. It was a menswear store last time I paid any attention to it.

O'Malleys' gradual demise was no more pleasant. Its final incarnation was narrow, dark and rather dingy.

I've a vague memory of Patrick Walker and I sharing drinks and conversation there – he still has the framed shirt has Dad bought him on the 2001 Crawl and yes, he does now appreciate the gesture.

I think we were missing a couple of regular Crawlers in Alastair and Colleen because both were involved in a Discworld play at the Arts Theatre that night. Not a good idea to turn up for a performance after spending the day visiting pubs – the temptation to have "just a couple of drinks" would be very hard to ignore!

.o0o.

43 2017 – MY DRY RUN

Once again Gregor bravely put his hand up to work out the route. For the purposes of posterity, here is the 'scouting report' he prepared from his reconnaissance with his mate Brett.

1. CRITERION. 10.00am. Pint Coopers green.

Brett arrived about 10.20 and said he needed to go to his bank in Indooroopilly. So really number two was the Pig and Whistle - pot of Tooheys New.

2. BEACH HOUSE. 11.25. Bottle Coopers Red.
3. EMBASSY. 11.55. Pot of Stout.
4. STOCK EXCHANGE. 12.10. Pot Carlton Mid. By-passed the Victory. Too noisy. And time restraints.
5. MR EDWARDS. 12.25. Coopers Stout Schooner. Pretty German barmaid.
6. PORT OFFICE. 12.50. Schooner Kosciuszko.

Ferry.

7. STORY BRIDGE. 1.27. Back on schedule. Pot Hass L Hop.

Taxi. (Bus once per hour)

8. PINEAPPLE. 1.50. Schooner Kosciuszko.
9. GERMAN CLUB. 2.30. 2 x Landbier Dunkel and 1/2 Herring Salad.
10 WOOLLOONGABBA. 3.15. Bottle Coopers Red.
11. BREWHOUSE. Ex CLARENCE CORNER. 3.40. By-passed the MORRISON due to time restraints. Pint of Stout.
12. SHIP INN. 4.15. Coopers Green. Herewith the scout ended. We retired to West End.

For the Crawl itself on October 14 I think that both the Victory and the Morrison were added back onto the list. The 'back end' after the Ship took us to the Plough and the Fox before crossing the bridge back to the Criterion.

The Pineapple was at last on the list, to Lurch's delight. The fitter ones walked. Some lucked onto a bus and some shared taxis and minivans.

The distance between numbers 7, 8 and 9 on Gregor's list was a source of some complaint from some, admittedly. "We're not as young as we used to be," and "We're walking *how* far?!" Certainly, we haven't been as ambitious in subsequent years, even though I did enjoy taking Eric into the German Club just this once.

Yet another of Eric's cushions had disintegrated under the onslaught of his libations at each bar. So I devised something new – a natty, decorative black and white box that was padded and carefully lined with plastic. I figured that could be removed and replaced every year while the box remained intact. Theory worked out pretty well in practice, too, for the next three years.

The most memorable thing about the 2017 Eric for me is that this was the one year when I completed a Crawl having consumed little or no alcohol.

I don't especially want to go into detail – I still wince when I think about it. Let's just say there had been surgery, uncomfortable enough in its own right, complicated further by a post-operative infection. Uncomfortable, unpleasant, and requiring medication that severely limited the amount of alcohol that I could safely consume.

I reckon I had a gin and tonic to start the day, probably an interesting beer at the German Club, and maybe one other something along the way. But mostly it was variations on lime and soda.

So it was the remarkable year when I stayed sober. That gave me a new and different perspective on everyone else's behaviour, and yes it was still fun.

 I do still wonder though if perhaps my usual regime of gin and tonics would have created a more antiseptic environment and kept me infection-free.

.o0o.

44 2018 – SO NEAR AND YET SO FAR

It's ridiculous that as I write this it's less than a year since 13 October, 2018 and yet I have less memory of the Crawl on that date than just about any other since 1979. Well, they do say it's the short term memory that's first to go.

Who are "they"? Umm... I don't recall.

I do know we started at the Criterion. Present at the Reserved Table for Gill's Old Bastards were (left to right in the photo:) Bushell, Anne Connell, Matt T., Matt W., Gav, Jill, Ian, Renoir, Gav, Lurch, Shaz, Gregor, Ern and Robbo.

I know there were eleven pubs visited, but I'd only be guessing at an actual itinerary. Pretty confident that we stuck to the CBD though – perhaps as a reaction to the tyranny of distance noted a year earlier.

Matt T. bailed after eight of those bars. He'd injured a knee and could barely walk. Six months later it was still giving him trouble.

Alastair was performing at the Arts again, I think, although I also recall drinks with Margaret and Madelaine at O'Malley's – possibly on their way to the show.

The Port Office was, I think, more crowded than usual. I'm not sure if there was a Function on, or if the place had just become more fashionable, but I remember little pockets of Pub Crawlers scattered about in a broader throng, like brightly coloured flowers in a dull rockery. A couple of us circulated like blood cells.

I remember Pimm's on tap at Gilhooley's being a surprise treat. I only bought a pint, but was impressed by the prospect of a jug. It's not like it's especially potent. Pleasantly fruity I suppose is how I'd describe it. But it always makes me think of a particularly grand day in England. Meredith and I attended the Gloucester Motor Show with my cousin and her husband, both dear friends. It was in the grounds of some Stately Home, but as well as the fabulous vintage cars on display we all enjoyed multiple drinks from the very genteel Pimms tent that had been set up in the gardens.

Bushell is an important figure in Pub Crawling history, being one of the originals from the early Walks Against Thirst in Sydney. A few regulars from the event have made it up to join Eric. And not surprisingly, quite a few Friends Of Eric have participated in the annual Crawl around the Rocks. Sharon has become a regular there, and at different times there have been appearances by Megan, Judy, Karl and Renoir. I've yet to take Eric on that particular adventure, though.

During the course of the Crawl we (Shaz, Gav and I, maybe) realised that Easter Saturday in 2019 just happened to coincide with the demolition of the Belle Vue. So, giving everyone present plenty of warning, we announced the forthcoming date for Eric's 40th – April 20.

Maybe I'd learned something from the 2017 'sober' Eric, because as the day wore on I was better than I'd ever been at interspersing some 'light' choices amongst my regular gin and tonics. I may not have been under .05 by the end of the Crawl but I was more lucid than on many previous occasions. Like the previous year I found myself more aware of my surroundings.

Noticed, too what other people (not just Friends of Eric) were doing. Their reactions to us, and particularly Eric, were mostly in the range from amused to bemused. Some ignored or didn't notice us, and a very few harrumphed, muttered or growled. Sod 'em, as Robbo would say.

I know I drove home after breakfast the next day, and I don't believe it was misplaced confidence. I've made that dumb mistake before, and learned my lesson.

.o0o.

45 2019 – THE FORTIETH ANNIVERSARY

 2019 has proved to be a year of auspicious anniversaries for our favourite Pub Crawl. Four decades since the demolition of the Belle Vue, but also forty years since the release of *Monty Python's Life of Brian*, which gave us one of the great anthems as Friends of Eric do tend to always look on the bright side of life. In a similar vein, this year marks the fiftieth anniversary of the television debut of *Monty Python's Flying Circus*. (Although the *Eric the Half A Bee* song didn't appear until November 1972 – who called me a trivia buff?)

 There were supposed to be commemorative t-shirts, just as there'd been a decade earlier. A plain white t-shirt emblazoned with a photo of the Belle Vue in her glory days. A couple of people who ordered them actually *got* their shirt in time for the Crawl. For a number of others, it would be an opportunity to resuscitate a favourite shirt from years gone by (and in some cases, skite about still fitting into it, eh Marc?).

 Capricious fate had it that the fortieth anniversary of the Deen Brothers starting up their engines of destruction fell on Easter Saturday. That added to the 'holiday spirit' of the event, but also cost us quite a number of otherwise keen starters.

 There was a problem at the planning stage – nobody was able to do a proper reconnoiter of what pubs would be open and when on what was, nominally at least, a public holiday. Megan, Sharon and Gregor all found some info, as did a small scouting party of Lurch, Alastair, Bernard and me. But all those composite bits didn't add up to much.

 So for the first time in forty years: a whole new strategy. Nominate a starting pub, and then a route, rather than a real 'itinerary'.

 I'd had the notion to recreate the 79 trail as much as possible. That fell at the first hurdle. The Queenslander Bar in the Transit Centre has closed (another one bites the dust) and the Transcontinental owners didn't want to pay penalty rates to the staff over Easter so weren't opening. The Grosvenor has just closed, so the first open pub on George Street at 10:00 am wound up being the Criterion anyway. That's actually pretty cool, since it's the home of Gill's Old Bastards.

The starters joining Eric on this auspicious occasion were Anthony, Dallas, Eleanor, Ern, Funsize, Gav, Gregor, Ian & his sister Alison, Karl, Leanne, Lurch & Jill, Marc, Matt & Caitlin, Matt W., Megan & Doug, Paul K, Renoir, Shaz, and Wayne H.

Apologies were received from Budgie, Judy, Robbo, Buddy, Danielle and Meredith. Not just for purely historical reasons I'd have loved to have them with us, along with many others fondly remembered from the forty year history who didn't respond to their invitations. But if wishes were horses we'd all be Bart Cummings, and I'm very, very happy to have shared the day with the people who were there.

It's a continuing delight to me that Ern has made the effort to front up for the first bar or two for so many years. His health hasn't always been great but he's been there anyway. I think – I *hope* he knows how much I appreciate that. It's never a long enough conversation, but it's always a good one.

Actually, that last sentence holds true for many of the regular Crawlers. An Eric is a great opportunity to catch up with people, but the continuous movement of bodies usually means that conversations are fragmented, and sometimes opportunities for a long chat are scarce.

To honour the anniversary event, Lurch composed a new Ode, roughly to the tune of the old *Half A Bee* song:
>Half a brick, to the philosophic, is ipso facto half not brick.
>But Half-A-Brick to the historic, is The Belle Vue, sul generis, metonymic.

(That means that Eric's 'surname' is uniquely associated with the Belle Vue to the point where his name is used when talking about the pub. As in: The Eric Memorial Crawl.)

Sometimes, my old mate Lurch's literary and linguistic skills lead to offerings that can be a bit... obtuse. Certainly, he'd be well suited to some of the great 'writer's pubs' to be found on a Crawl around Dublin's Temple Bar. Rosco and I did that trip some years ago, and a few of us discussed it longingly at the Mall version of the Pig & Whistle.

Quite early on Matt W. made the observation to me that, "Eric's red bits are going grey – not unlike your good self." Sadly, I couldn't argue with that.

As we walked we added the Grand Central to our itinerary, although it's not on the streets originally listed. The simple reason being, we knew it was open!

While there, a few of us were discussing the last four decades of Eric's history. The Frozen Broccoli Award was mentioned, I won't say 'fondly'. Marc remarked that "we're all getting to an age where stumbling is more of a pastime than an infrequency". Nodding, Lurch added, "And the consequences are more severe."

Disappointed to find the Gresham not opening until 4:00 pm. Disappointed because although the building is different (the bar is in the old National Bank HQ on Queen Street) it adjoins the site of the original Gresham, which had just missed being on the 1979 list by being demolished not long before. And *especially* disappointed because only a couple of weeks earlier the staff assured me they were opening at 11:00 am on Easter Saturday.

Walking down Creek Street, several of us saw a sign for a bar no-one recognised, but in large friendly letters said, "We serve salad!" That put most people off, but I saw the words 'Sports Bar' and chose to ignore the salad. Matt W., Eric and I turned out to be the only Crawlers to visit the small but interesting Sports Bar. I hope it's a stayer.

Clanc turned up at the Grand Central, only a few hours late, then decided it was too wet to go any further. Well, he's out of practice at the whole Pub Crawl thing...

Funsize departed in time to fly overseas, setting some sort of new record for waking up the morning after a Crawl by doing so in Amsterdam.

After Friday's came the Riverside Bar, dismissed or ignored by some as being "not interesting enough" – not sure when that became a criterion for inclusion. Personally I liked the view, and some of the more imaginative suggestions of how 'Felon Brewing' across the river got its name. Most plausible, I thought, was a link to the old Water Police site. "They stole the recipe and/or the yeast" wasn't a bad one either.

And then came the Bavarian, omitted by several of us on the understanding that the place is a restaurant, and we didn't want to order a meal just to have a beer.

In the Pav it was learned to be careful when you order: one gin and tonic, in a small glass, cost Karl $15. Doug paid $8 for a g & t in a tall glass – clearly you need to confirm which shelf you want the gin to come from. The Pav was also where Gregor slipped away. With some surgery looming on his horizon, he's being more aware of his health than on some past occasions. The stroke of 2000 remains the most emphatic Frozen Broccoli Award ever announced, etched in a lot of memories.

There was intermittent drizzle all day. After a few pubs, no-one really noticed much, and as Karl observed, "it was never going to be a dry day anyway".

But there were occasional downpours. We got the edge of one between the Pig & Whistle and Grand Central, but mostly missed the worst of the weather, like when we left the Pavilion just as the rain stopped. Marc observed that Eric must have friends in high places. The Pav was where Rosco joined us after spending the morning playing in a golf tournament. Another good walk ruined.

At the Buffalo Bar there was a little split between inside and out. No ill-feelings or tensions, just some people having more of a desire for fresh air than others, and it did turn out to be one of the afternoon's dry spells.

Another new arrival on the Brisbane bar scene turned out to be the Doo Bop Bar – a very appealing 'jazz joint'. Several of us had initially walked past it, but some of the trailing crew couldn't resist and when they caught up at the Victory, waxed so lyrical about it that a quick 'catch-up' was called for.

It was worth the temporary chaos. An excellent range of drinks at not too unreasonable prices, and a really good ambience to the place. There was only one Crawler unimpressed. He somehow was convinced that the place was a front for the Russian mafia, and that the two guys on staff were "dangerous". I'm not going to say who that was, just on the remote possibility that he was right.

The Victory beer garden, probably now the best in Brisbane (umm... maybe the only one?), distinguished itself by offering $10 jugs of a range of beers. They were sufficiently good value to tempt several of us who were otherwise consistent gin and tonic drinkers.

I will admit to also getting a kick out of the MMA bout (pardon the pun) on one of the pub TV screens. That's Mixed Martial Arts, for those of you who've led sheltered lives. It was a Classic Bout – i.e. an old one being replayed, between Brock Lesnar and Alex Overeem. Lesnar has also been a prominent pro wrestler, and is for many reasons a man I really don't like. So I enjoyed seeing Overeem get a very dominant win in quick time. Call it a little guilty pleasure.

The Stock Exchange was another one that wasn't opening until too late - 6:00pm, but frankly, not one that was much missed. Ditto the Embassy, which didn't open at all.

As we walked up Elizabeth Street Rosco looked up and noticed a young lady wandering around in her first floor apartment, which had a glass wall that fronted the street. She wasn't naked straight from the shower, as some thought or suggested (a trick of the light). There was a lot of stopping, gazing and waving. None of this was noticed, or at least reacted to by the woman in question. Well spotted, Rosco, and a salient reminder of why some of us really don't like that sort of architectural feature.

Pimm's was on tap at Gilhooley's again, this time a jug of it was shared by me, Karl, Alastair and Bernard. It was also where we lost Lurch who had a very good excuse: there was no way he could be late for the dinner to celebrate his Mum's eighty-somethingth birthday!

There was a little ceremony of remembrance at the Belle Vue site. I was intrigued to discover that the glass and steel building that eventually replaced the pub has been demolished, thus lasting less time than the Crawl. A little win. In attendance were Karl, Wayne & Anne (thanks for the beers Anne!), Leanne and Martin, an overseas visitor she 'found' in Irish Murphy's.

In Irish Murphy's, Rosco was delighted at St. Kilda's 40 point win over Melbourne, and grateful for not hearing the leaving "Yooo!" until the final siren!

Somehow in various ways we lost Dallas, Gav, Chris and Leanne between Murphy's and the Cri.

So after all that, the itinerary as it finally happened was:

Criterion	Pig & Whistle (Mall)	Grand Central
Sports Bar	Pig & Whistle (Riverside)	Friday's
Riverside	Bavarian	Pavilion
Buffalo	Doo Bop	Victory
Gilhooley's	Irish Murphy's	Criterion

Last survivors: Ian, Kelly Anne, Renoir, Karl, Rosco, Shaz, Ruth, Al, Bernard, Bushell, Legend, Upright, Dave, Megan, Doug, Matt W., Marc, Paul K. And of course Eric, although his box wasn't going to last much longer!

Upright is another campaigner from the Walk Against Thirst, although she makes her home in Hobart these days. She and partner Dave happened to be visiting Brisbane at a *very* convenient time, and they were welcome Eric debutantes.

Alastair's son Bernard also made his adult debut, and fitted in like a bum in a bucket. He and his Pa were there for most of the Crawl through to the end: amiable company and suitably fond of a drink and good conversation. Maybe I've just had a glimpse of the future.

Rosco's thoughts on the day: "I came. I saw. I had a few drinks. I went home. Arriving half way through has elements of being both a blessing and a curse, like being sober enough at the Pavilion to notice the prices. The jazz bar we found (*Doo Bop*) was impressive."

Karl's observation was that it seemed a bit more chaotic than his previous experiences, mostly because of the 'route but no itinerary' approach, but that's not necessarily a bad thing. Most important was that the whole day was very convivial!

Between can-rattling and t-shirts we pulled in $120. Not too shabby for a good cause.

All in all, another successful day – and in deference to those who couldn't make it along because of Easter, there will be a sequel.

Eric 40.5 will happen in November, only the second ever 'supplementary' Crawl. Eric will be there, and I expect so will I.

There's a tradition to maintain…

.o0o.

46 Not A Conclusion

No, 'conclusion' is definitely the wrong word.

We're not planning to stop after forty years. Plans are useless but planning is essential, said Dwight D. Eisenhower, apparently. So we are planning to not stop.

How we continue, where, when and who will be part of Crawls to come – all of those questions will resolve themselves in time. The important thing is that those who attend continue to have fun.

Dallas has been a part of most of the Crawls since the formation of Gill's Old Bastards (I think he missed one when he had to be at work). He offered his thoughts on what he likes about the annual event:
> "It's the family get-together that you actually *want* to attend. Catch up with people you haven't seen for a year, and some you've seen too often during the year but you don't care. You get along with everyone, and if there's someone you don't, you go find someone you do. After a few drinks you do get along anyway. I love it."

I guess by now the number of people who've been a part of at least one Eric The Half-A-Brick Testimonial Pub Crawl is well into the hundreds. Many have made fleeting appearances, some more memorable than others. Many have been stayers. All have been friends, and appreciated and valued as such.

There are those who we know we won't see again, in this life anyway, like Rocky, Alex and I'm sure others who's passing I've not known about.

I've just been looking at a 2003 photo that includes Tony, Filthy and Gill, and missing all of them. But we go on, I go on, and Eric goes on.

We'll raise a glass to them and other absent friends every year, and continue on our merry way, partying and enjoying the company of those around us, old friends and new, just as they would do.

If you're reading this, there's a very good chance you've been a part of Eric's journey. Thank you for that. If you've never undertaken the trip with us, then you're welcome – and encouraged – to correct that oversight. Brisbane's best mobile party awaits you.

If I was compiling for Eric one of the old-style 'mixed tapes' that we used to present each other with, there are a few songs I'd have to include, besides the *Half-a-Bee Song* and *Gilligan's Island*.
The Travelling Wilburys' *When The Walls Came Down.*
The Beatles' *With A Little Help From My Friends*
George Thorogood's *One Bourbon, One Scotch and One Beer*
Jimi Hendrix's *Purple Haze*
Status Quo's *I Don't Remember Any More*
And of course the Beach Boys' *Let's Do It Again.*

Yes. Let's. I'll drink to that.

.xXx.